TALES
FOR MY
BROTHERS'
KEEPERS

TALES FOR MY BROTHERS' KEEPERS

BY

THOMAS FLYNN

W · W · NORTON & COMPANY · INC ·

New York

Published simultaneously in Canada
by George J. McLeod Limited, Toronto

Library of Congress Cataloging in Publication Data
Flynn, Thomas, 1944–
    Tales for my brothers' keepers.
    1. Flynn, Thomas, 1944– 2. Prisoners—Personal narratives. I. Title.
HV9468.F6A34   1976   365'.6'0924   75-45157
ISBN 0-393-07502-8

This book was designed by Jacques Chazaud
Typefaces used were Deepdene and Electra
Manufactured by Vail-Ballou Press, Inc.

Printed in the United States of America

1 2 3 4 5 6 7 8 9 0

For Martin, Al, and Phil. You kept me alive.

The initial shiver of inspiration was prompted by a story about an ape who produced the first drawing ever charcoaled by an animal: this sketch showed the bars of the poor creature's cage.

—Nabokov, *Lolita*

ह्ब

His vision from the passing of the bars
is grown so weary that it holds no more.
To him it seems there are a thousand bars
and behind a thousand bars no world.

The padding gait of flexibly strong strides,
that in the very smallest circle turns,
is like a dance of strength around a center
in which stupefied a great will stands.

Only sometimes the curtain of the pupil
soundlessly parts—. Then an image enters,
goes through the tensioned stillness of the limbs—
and in the heart ceases to be.

—Rilke

ह्ब

This life appears unbearable; another unattainable. One is no longer ashamed of wanting to die, one asks to be moved from the old cell, which one hates, to a new one, which one will only in time come to hate. In this there is also a residue of belief that during the move the master will chance to come along the corridor, look at the prisoner and say: "This man is not to be locked up again. He is come to me."

—Kafka

❦

Foreword

We know very little about this young man the older inmates call "kid," neither the circumstances of his conviction (beyond the fact that it was a "drug bust"), nor the prison he's doing his time in.

He tells us only that he was young "during 1969 and 1970, years blown large with the wild promise of freedom even as they were dominated by war and repression. . . . Sharing a common exhilaration, open to almost any possibility—the larger community clearly insane—we began to shape new lives. We saw ourselves as both outlaws and pioneers, crossing uncharted and often dangerous terrain. . . . Yet even as I repudiated the past, hurling onward, it took more phlegm than I possessed not to be dizzied by the urgency of so many new imperatives . . . straining to stay abreast of the madness, theirs and ours, unable to ease the pace, I became a daredevil. . . . Even as I was incarcerated by a lunatic society, I found myself guilty of selling short the best aspirations of our new life."

But this is enough to tell us that he was middle class, educated, receptive to the world around him, exceptionally able to translate his perceptions into words. In

9

short, he is not like most prison inmates ("Hope to die," says Shorty, another inmate, "if that boy ain't a writin' fool. . . . Look at him go . . . you tell me there aren't all different ways to do time.") and therefore he is able to give us, as most inmates could not, this unforgettable picture of prison time, how men do it, what it does to them.

Tales for My Brothers' Keepers is not an institutional or scholarly book, nor is it a book of protest and demands for reform. It is a book about men, lives, moments. It makes its statement in the quiet tones of a dreamer murmuring in sleep ("Another gray winter morning, sky low over the prison, only three hundred and four days till Christmas."). It is unsentimental (except about radical youth), unemotional, often unbearable. Here, for only one example, is a description of what happened to another young inmate who had been urged to fight back against the sexual advances of a tough con named Max.

"In the shower room several nights later, what Max drove on him, the boy picked up a chair and tried to shield himself. Max ripped the chair away, took a bar of soap in his fist, knocked the boy across the face with the back of his hand, smeared some soap on his penis, and entered the boy from behind as the boy lay sprawled face down on the shower-room floor."

That is one of the realities of prison and here is another: "Dreams aside, I'm worn with the grayness of each slow hour, ground down by the noise, the routine, and the violence. I find myself slipping out of control, losing hold, backpedaling, now only reacting . . ."

Men reach prison by all routes. Carl, who is doing "a nickel" for dealing cocaine, got there because his partner turned out to be a narc. And "the kid" listens with interest as "a dentist serving six months for tax evasion describes his system for handling three patients simultaneously. An extortionist–gun runner shares with me cheeses he has bribed a guard to smuggle in for him. Giving me a cigar, he tells me—'in strictest confidence' —of secret meetings with Duvalier. And a stock manipulator recounts the beauties of his mistress. 'You're never too old for it, kid, believe me,' he says. He then explains how he has appealed for reduction of his three-month sentence by pleading the need to be at the side of his ailing wife."

However they get there, however they choose to do their time ("I can occupy myself," says Frank, explaining to the Captain why he refuses to take a prison job; after that, he occupies himself in segregation), all prison inmates are subject to the same excruciating boredom, the same mindless regimentation and petty tyranny, the ever-present threat of violence, the unbearable drag of time. Even the guards—themselves doing time, the cons like to say—are in much the same condition. One guard, nicknamed Absurdo, for example, "feels for the men. Intuitively he understands that he could be in their place, but is not threatened by the thought."

For the fact is that "Absurdo hasn't had much freedom, no time to explore, just school, the service, marriage, children, and the first government job that required nothing more than a high-school diploma. Two weeks off a year, three after another five years on the job, Absurdo knows about being institutionalized, he knows about time."

Behind the walls, the most momentous outside event

can have vastly different meaning. Gathered with the other inmates in the unusual experience of watching television an hour and a half after the usual lockup, the author watches Americans land on the moon and reflects: "The glare of the guard lights on the walls is so strong that only the moon is bright enough to be seen in the night sky. Until tonight it was free, well beyond our lives, we could follow its changes, and through it transcend our limits here below. Though stars hold so much more possibility, it was the moon alone which was beyond man's reach and still visible to us. Now man is there, the Man, of all men to have made it."

He resents the fact that the moon exploit "renders my fixed universe relatively smaller." But the fact that it *was* a small universe in itself, like nothing outside, like nothing most of us have seen or ever will, gave "the kid" his special opportunity. No doubt he would prefer not to have had it but, given no choice, he did not miss his moment. He has told us as much of what prison is like as anyone could, this "writin' fool" scribbling away his time, and he has told us, as a result, that "this concrete tomb for the living" dishonors us all.

TOM WICKER

TALES
FOR MY
BROTHERS'
KEEPERS

*H*ere, now, spring advancing into summer, winter's cold rains suddenly no more than a memory, I'm startled from a daydream to discover myself finally and irrevocably no longer young. Commencing my twenty-ninth circuit of the sun, even as yet another yellow rose unfurls, I turn into the house to sequester myself from such inexorable blooming.

So much time has passed. Now, if only for this moment of transition, it is the time behind me I feel. One must decide how to deal with it, one could sort the past not at all or forever sift, weigh, unravel. I have trunks full of the past, packages and packets packed with the past.

God knows I'm glad to be rid of February's pallid sun. I feel the shoots' thrust, my heart sings, of course these migrations draw me onward. But still I find myself retracing steps already taken, I wander paths that are vanished, but familiar.

How to view this past? I know far too many revisionist historians eager for respite, lurching past certificates of birth, death, and separation, in danger of forgetting their very names. Reducing what was to what might have been, shaken to discover the limits of their strength, some dreamers only dimly recall their vectors, they question their own force, they doubt their direction.

Loath to harden my heart, I want to anneal the past, to burn it bright as life itself. Dimming this time, surely it will be proof against shattering. Or, perhaps, the past will simply lay itself to rest like a dog circling for sleep, round, round, and down.

ॐ

The stories that follow are set in this so often savage country during 1969 and 1970, years blown large with the wild promise of freedom even as they were dominated by war and repression. This was a time of soldiers and police, demonstrators, freaks, and dreamers.

Having sped through a series of epiphanies about our society, both inspired by the palpable joy of discovery and full of regret that I had been so slow to learn, I, like some others, came to think of myself as beyond the social contract. Sharing a common exhilaration, open to almost any possibility—the larger community clearly insane—we began to shape new lives. We saw ourselves as both outlaws and pioneers, crossing uncharted and often dangerous terrain. As the poet says, "There was music in the cafés at night and revolution in the air."

So there I was, young and crazy, hungry and wild, a singer of songs. Coming alive. Laughing at and being overwhelmed by the magic, humor, and vertigo of this world being born.

16

Yet even as I repudiated the past, hurling onward, it took more phlegm than I possessed not to be dizzied by the urgency of so many new imperatives. There were no boundaries. Having constantly to redefine truth and necessity—how many revolutions were there?—straining to stay abreast of the madness, theirs and ours, unable to ease the pace, I became a daredevil. And then, losing my "one point," not "together," I "blew it." Even as I was incarcerated by a lunatic society, I found myself guilty of selling short the best aspirations of our new life. "Peace is here if you want it," they were singing, but I had not found my way.

Given the bitterness of conflict in this country, 1969 had to be the wrong time to enter prison. The current prison reform movement was not then substantial, and few free men and women identified what oppressed them with the force that kept others behind bars. Nor, with the exception of the Black Muslims, were there organized alternatives to the roles of predator and victim which defined traditional prison life. The society still freely abused its prisoners, even as the prisoners themselves, in almost timeless isolation, freely abused each other.

This was before Soledad, when a guard was killed in retaliation for the murder of an inmate, and before Attica, when inmates protesting dreadful conditions were shot down like dogs. As late as 1969 the struggles rending the country affected institution life only by making prison authorities more devoted to crushing dissent.

For me incarceration was nearly incomprehensible, not only because I knew nothing of prisons, but because before being confined I had tasted such raw energy, bounty, and shared exuberance. So recent were the revelations and changes that from inside it was often difficult to trace the steps that had brought me there. Bereft, I had only my fulfillment of one of the negative possibilities of that new world, and the promise of martyrdom if I lived by its terms within the walls.

Of course there were ties to bind. At first I shared news of the outside as though I was only temporarily absent from it. Friends who had once looked to me to test the limits of their new freedom now waited for me to escape from prison, laugh at it, or somehow subsume it. And, initially, it was true: incarceration only advanced my appreciation of what we had been living, it only increased my desire to shrug off all restraints.

As prison slowly dulled my senses, however, and as for me the prison universe was ever more total, those outside increasingly spoke to me of what constrained them. Obligation, illness, heartbreak, failure of the imagination; stories of prisons less literal than my own became our common ground.

These bonds notwithstanding, life as I had known it was the more remote because no friends outside understood the specifics of prison's deprivations and terrors. In censored letters, and in too brief visits, until, psychologically, I could no longer negotiate the passage out to the free world and back in three hours a month, I labored to communicate the reality of prison to those who spoke my language.

These two worlds—between which I felt myself the only thread—were in turn irreconcilable with the world

I confronted the day I stepped off the bus wearing a prison suit, white shirt, and tie, hair cropped and face shaven clean. Longhairs around the station, eying someone so "straight," appraised me carefully. Already I felt beyond the alternatives available in such Manichean times.

So long out of place, I had immediately to wash the prison from my soul. But how was I to rejoin the living when even the stalwart were blown out of shape by the sheer speed of so many cataclysms? And, full of rage and sadness, how was I to catch up to the crazed exhilaration all around me?

With the help of my friends I rediscovered laughter, and, slowly, opened my heart. In time good fortune carried me forward. I watched stalking fishermen cast hand nets at fish sighted in the curl of breaking waves. And, once, I became the point on which the whole damn ocean converged as, shrieking with laughter, a friend was millraced from tidepool to tidepool.

Still there were circles to close. For me prison's special cruelty was in rendering men incapable of appreciating their suffering for what it was, and, worse, unable to imagine alternatives to it. More, since one concealed a prison record to "make it" in the free world, prisoners understood that they would continue to have a stake in suppressing feelings of what was experienced inside. "If you look back, you're coming back," went the jailhouse expression.

As I looked back, my perspective was necessarily oblique, if only because I could not take on all that sadness a second time. I came rather to think of making a landscape of those lives and that time, to in layers super-impose one fragment on another until, with accretion, the terrain would emerge.

჻

Even as the inside became a function of memory, I connected with its living reality through four men I had know well within the walls. Al, a steady and true friend inside, a black man of enormous potential and great anger, located me shortly after he got out. He needed help.

One day we went to a park for a swim. Overwhelmed with the ease of the day and the self-reliant grace of the two women who accompanied us, Al said little, content to listen to the talk. At one point, finishing a beer, he crumpled the can in his fist, and, done with it, tossed it behind him on the ground. Seeing this, the women were dismayed, while Al, reading their faces, was hurt. Trying to be "cool," he was way behind the times. Too much of his youth spent in prison, himself seldom the object of solicitude, it had never occurred to him that the environment was something to protect.

As time passed he continued to find too subtle the world he had yearned to join when within the walls. Wearied by repeated gaffes, judging himself unfit for freedom, he committed a small and forlornly unsuccessful burglary and was returned inside.

My jailhouse friend Pete, a draft resister, emerged from a prison term he had endured with equanimity to wander Europe and the States, covering miles, picking up threads of the past. Locating a quiet place to light, finally, but then uprooted, suddenly finding the world too vast, discovering in himself a need for structure that prison had no doubt reinforced, he returned to his home town. With wry appreciation for the humor of this long deferred yet now imperative reunion with convention, nevertheless going all the way back to go, he resumed, with relief, the undergraduate career he had repudiated eight years earlier.

Lefty, who at long last made his way out to a halfway house, quickly learned the ropes of the free world, sometimes too skillfully, taking jailhouse techniques out to the street, always wary, never giving too much of himself away. Still and all, he did make it.

But it was Martin who, after serving three years for possession of marijuana, set out to rejoin the counterculture. Flush times, however, were long gone; over and again he and his newfound ol' lady had to scuffle on the street. But then one evening Martin docked their battered school bus–starship off the Great Highway at land's end in San Francisco. The full moon rose over Mount Davidson, the egg-yolk sun eased into the horizon, and migrating birds pushed north over the waves of his new back yard.

It was a marginal livelihood, food stamps and odd jobs, but by making a vocation of being on the periphery Martin gained running room, and was entitled to some divine madness. He came to think of himself as caretaker of the beach, gathering trash as a public service. Improvising lyrics to familiar tunes, he once sang: "I'm so free, I'm so free, picking up garbage by the edge of the sea."

Stigmatized by time inside, however, Martin increasingly countered temporal impotence with assertions of spiritual power. As the hip scene vanished, as he confronted the risks of autism, he could not retreat, so he advanced. Martin from Mars, galactic courier, and his macramé spaceship. "I'm doin' good, and good is all I'm doin'," he would say, when asked how he was. Or, speaking of city officials, "They acknowledge me for what I am, and I have their good graces, since money relates to money, and dignity to dignity."

Being central to the universe made Martin too needy of confirmation, but it had its serendipities. Describing a bureaucrat with whom he was negotiating his rights to the beach, grinning with surprise at his own words, he said, "I believe her, on good authority, to be the mayor's ex-wife, and of course the mayor is a glutton."

One autumn day—six weeks before time as we know it was to come to an end, according to Martin's calendar—a city cop spotted Martin and told him to move his bus from the beach parking lot. Health code regulations. Martin protested, vehemently, that the beach was his. Why should he move? Irritated, suddenly seeing in Martin's wild eyes and long hair a latter-day Manson, the patrolman clubbed him down. Bloodied, Martin struggled to his knees, grabbed the patrolman, and dragged him twenty feet to the windbreak of potted plants he called his victory garden.

And that was it. Assault on an officer. County jail. Starship impounded. Food rotting. Ol' lady on the streets. Desperate calls to relatives and friends. Again the morass.

Now more than ever Martin could not abandon his task. "You know me for what I am, Thomas," he said. "I've waited till the very last moment. I want to accomplish what I came here to do. The time has come."

At a hearing on reduction of his bail, bringing up the rear of a day-long column of whores, thieves, vagrants, and drunks, immediately preceded by a shoplifter who identified himself as Zorro's younger brother, Martin stood before a judge who, since the shootout at nearby Marin County Courthouse, had packed a pistol under his robes. To this uneasy and exhausted jurist Martin quoted, eyes blazing, from Matthew 13:

> You will listen and listen, but not understand;
> you will look and look, but not see,
> because this people's minds are dull
> and they have stopped up their ears,
> and they have closed their eyes . . .

For a long moment the judge wavered. Was Martin an eccentric good for local color, or, with that edge of apocalyptic menace, was he someone to watch out for? As the judge was thinking it through, the mother of a boy he had earlier remanded to custody began to sob loudly. The judge had had enough. It was the bitter end of a day packed with broken lives, he could just as easily have let the woman's son go, so he did what he could at the moment—he released Martin without bail.

Outside the courtroom Martin was jubilant. A miracle, and all his own doing. Now they knew who he was! That he was broke, his bus impounded, that his public defender had no hope of beating the charges, none of this was real to him as he exulted in his victory.

३✥

Like Al, Martin is still inside. While these four lives continue to touch my own, and in some way speak for it, the prison time we shared is ever more remote. So too are those years when so much of what was best was either against the law or against the wishes of those in power. The strife and lyricism of that time have been transformed, as have the melody and outrage with which I hurled myself into—and, barely, through—prison. A war is over. Neither apocalypse nor revolution has redeemed us. The Dionysian power of those days is contained, almost as if it never was. Those passions pass to the boundaries of imagining. New and pragmatic concerns become our realities. Nothing remains the same.

Now I let this go. Prison has long since taken too much of the time of my life. And already, really, it is just short of being once and for all too late to look back. The tide of freedom sweeps me onward, onward. Only an edge of fear remains, that, were I returned inside, it would immediately be as though I had never left.

As you for a moment enter this bitter universe, think of my friends, still inside, right now. And think of me, blessed with the freedom they are denied, "on the streets" and "in the wind."

F iling through a series of windowless corridors behind the courtroom to a holding cell, bird cage for our swan songs, we face the wall which separates prisoners from the free (walnut panel for them, concrete for us). Just through the door theater is in progress, and lawyers dart back and forth with last-minute changes in the script.

Costumed to look like guards, stage managers request that no one use the toilet, lest sounds of flushing disturb the principals on the other side of the wall. Every so often one of us is brought in from the wings, guided through a cameo role, and ushered off. Spoken for, mute, unwilling to make a scene, we play our parts.

Men shoot in and out of the holding cell like shuttlecocks, each the messenger of bad tidings to his own kingdom. One gets a "nickel," another a "dime," and unless there is some too cruel effort to break through the language that saves, unless it is insisted that in this figure of speech each penny is a year of life, then it can be said in good faith: "Shit, man, ain't nothin', do it standin' on your hands."

As we are led to another cell, roar of commuter traffic

surging up from the freeway below, the guard folds back his sleeves to show that he wears no watch. Don't ask him about time. We reach the cell, take our first steps forward on the straight and narrow we've been admonished to follow, and the cell door slams shut behind us.

Piss-stained mattresses, no sheets, no pillows, no towels, no books, nothing and nowhere to go. Still, we have our voices.

"You'll do more time than Big Ben, sucker."

"Don't ever play catch-up with a broad."

"Boy, you ain't never gettin' outta here."

"But, Your Honor!"

Down the line, guards beat a man in the solitary cell. "Don't kill me, please don't kill me," he cries. "I'm sorry, Mr. White Man, please stay, I'll tell you, just don't shut that door."

We sit silent, listening. Nobody wants to join him. Finally someone shouts, "Shut up, punk!" As if this voice which has spoken for us administers the final blow, the man is quiet.

In the hole cell next door, another prisoner breaks, reverting to boot-camp days, over and again singing out the digits of his dog-tag number, varying the speed and rhythm of the cadence as if trying to break its code, occasionally interrupting himself to scream, "Kill, kill, kill!" And then, resuming his efforts to fathom once and for all the essential and cleverly disguised meaning of the numbers, he begins to linger on one digit at a time, repeating each as if mesmerized, until, after a while, his passion spent, he too is silent.

2 6

Later, losing control behind the solid metal door, he works desperately to engage another voice, calling out random words, place names, slogans, anything to interest or anger enough to draw human response. No one picks up on his gambits.

Finally, in a frenzy, he becomes a pilot on a mission, and takes off. "Pilot to bombardier, pilot to bombardier, come in please, come in please." Suddenly he draws fire. "We're hit, we're hit!" he screams, even as a new voice responds, "Bombardier to pilot, bombardier to pilot, come in please, pirates at four o'clock, pirates at four o'clock." The enemy is engaged.

Safe from the very worst (IN CASE OF ATOMIC ATTACK DO NOT PANIC YOU ARE SAFER HERE THAN ON THE STREET, reads a sign on the wall), we sit in our cell rolling cigarettes, splitting matches to conserve our small supply, watching the day wane through the glazed windows, eating our last pieces of bread long before the glass turns black. Tired of pushups, we return to homilies and stories.

"Walk the middle, man, gotta choose. Walk both sides, gotta pay."

"Cop a plea, fool, this is dead time, no matter how you cut it."

"Sheuuut, anybody knows Federal time's easier than State time."

Tonight Ray performs, and we are lucky to have him in our cell. The man can rap. A car thief, he takes us through the thirty days of vertigo before the Feds found him hiding between two mattresses in his girl friend's bedroom. Snitched out by her fiancé. Just back from the beach. "Still wearin' a fuckin' bathin' suit, man, a fuckin' bathin' suit."

He takes us with him for an hour at a time, disgressing over and again from previous digressions, and why not, we're rich in time. Soon we shoot through the night in a stolen Grand Prix, stopping at five, ten, twenty Standard Oil stations to refuel with the hot credit card, charging tires and accessories to peddle in the next town, charging Ramada Inn rooms, charging even the generous tips to the bellboys.

And always we are back into the car, driving twenty-six thousand miles in thirty days, decals on the window to map the progress, another sign to record what town, what state, always more road before us, another gas station, one more Ramada Inn.

Or sitting on the bed, planning this time to take the TV too, hearing a knock on the door, and out the fire escape just in time, damn the bitch for paying for the candy bar with the credit card, no wonder they got suspicious. So back to the road, shit, let's head home, but even to keep our appointment with the Man we rush like hell, only the odometer to log how far, and the gas gauge to say it won't be forever.

Reaching a pit stop in his story, Ray falls back on his mattress. Once more we sit in silence. Guards pass, and pass again. The block is quiet, most of the three hundred men on this line are sleeping, but in our cell we have trouble facing the stillness.

Jackie ("call me Jackie Tattoo"), short, fat, and prematurely bald, tattoos on arms and chest, is now wide awake, certain that by this late hour he has held his tongue long enough to demonstrate impressive reticence. Sucking on a menthol cigarette, actually believing that there is something here to win, he wants to top Ray's tale.

Across the cell from Jackie, his arms folded tight, missing nothing that goes on, is the Samoan we call "Pineapple." Far from home, the only one of his kind in this place, wary of both blacks and whites, he wreathes his suspicion and fear in a tight smile. Pegging Pineapple as a Chicano, returning the smile he totally misreads, Jackie is encouraged to begin.

Nowhere else to go, we let him transport us to the East Coast, to Little Italy and visions of seventy-dollar shirts and three-hundred-dollar suits. We admire his mohair and satin, his silk and cashmere. He begins to tell us about the big boys, about watching them when he was a kid, wanting to work for them, with them. We come to understand that he had to christen himself with his moniker.

As he speaks, we learn that he pursued the whole movie, not knowing that the film was already cracked and chipped, the print fading, that the game was stocks, lawyers, forms, computers. Way too late he actually sought out the Life. Bars, babes, booze. Limousines, diamond rings, a name. Scams, capers, shysters, heists. Two-bit punks. All this bringing him the promise of the grail—the joint, the Big Time. "I wanna continue my higher education," he tells us, "know what I mean?"

To give us his dream, Jackie asks if we have seen Kirk Douglas in *The Brotherhood*. No one has. How to ex-

plain? So here, in the dead of night in a lousy jail, Jackie admits us to the vision that moves him by revealing the work of the Masters—he does imitations of Edward G. Robinson and James Cagney.

"This game ain't for guys who are soft."

"You can dish it out but you can't take it."

"Did you ever stop to think how you'd look with a lily in your hand?"

"Oh, Mother of Mercy, is this the end of Rico?"

Smiling shyly, Jackie awaits our response. Unable to play cop to his robber, we affirm him. "Run it, man, run it." Grinning, Jackie tells us that he has written his life story, *Memories of a Player*. It is to be made into a movie, he explains, which he envisions opening as a narrator, in "one of those Gangbuster kind of voices," intones Jackie's poem "The Running Gun."

> I rode out of San Francisco, goin' south to New
>   Mexico,
> I was runnin' dodgin' the FBI, left the town
>   that I love so.
> Far behind lay San Francisco, and the rep that
>   I had earned,
> All the warrants that were on me marked the
>   lessons I had learned.
>
> Many times I used a credit card for a place to
>   lay my head,
> And the nights were full of visions of the men
>   that I left dead.
> I couldn't take it any longer with the life that
>   I'd begun,

So I bid goodbye to the city and became the
    runnin' one.

I rode into Amarillo as the sun sank in the west.
And thought of San Francisco and the clubs I
    like the best.
Far behind lay San Francisco and the rep that
    I had earned,
All the warrants that were on me marked the
    lessons I had learned.

I had barely left my Caddy and my feet just
    touched the ground,
When a cold voice right behind me told me
    not to turn around.
He said he knew about them warrants, knew
    I was wanted by the law,
Challenged by that Federal man I turned
    around to draw.

I knew someday I'd meet him for his hand like
    lightnin' flashed.
My .38 stood in leather while his .45 tore its
    path.
Now the crowd is slowly gatherin' but my eyes
    are growin' dim,
And my thoughts return to Frisco and the girl
    who was so slim.

Oh, tell her please won't you mister, that she's
    still the only one,
But that a woman's love is wasted when she
    loves the runnin' gun.
Runnin' gun.

"That's really something," Ray says for us. "Far out." Pineapple smiles. The night is finally almost over, the windows begin to lighten, the trusty works his way down the line. We've made it through the darkness, and, worn as we are, the day will slide by. Between the screams and the silence we still are safe. Now, exhausted but bolstered by being alive enough to tell the story or to hear it told, we do not listen for the real sounds, the cracking of spines, the splintering of manhood. We sleep.

ॐ

I don't like Rags, but we could hardly be closer. Manacled together, his right hand and my left, we're wedged in the back seat of the marshal's car with two other prisoners. "You an' me's tight as the skin on a golf ball," Rags says, "tight as dick's hatband."

All the way down from county jail, ever since he learned that it's my first fall, he's been telling me horror stories, waiting for me to lose heart. Wedged too close to turn, I watch his thin face and greased pompadour in the driver's mirror. He even looks like a vulture, I don't want to believe him, but his words do have the ring of truth.

"Dope bust? Up to six?" He laughs. "Figure on doing all your time," he says, grinning, as an early spring rain pounds the roof of the car. "Figure on doing every bit of it. And then some."

ॐ

Frank is forever on his back, hands behind his head, staring at the ceiling. He seems never to leave his bunk, never even to shift his weight. It's true that he is sighted walking slowly to chow, apparently unconcerned that the best of what little is served will be gone long before he makes it through the line, and of course he is seen in the washroom cleaning himself at the circular metal trough after other men have finished. Yet no matter what the time of day, hard evidence to the contrary, he seems always to be on his bunk, eyes locked in a vacant and unblinking gaze which compels one to look up there for himself. There is, needless to say, nothing on the ceiling but dull-green institutional gloss, not even any interesting cracks or ridges Frank might be using as landmarks to map some journey through inner space.

It never fails to provoke, his way of just lying there, perhaps because with such economy he disengages himself from the flow of life in the dormitory. The fifty men around him never cease to vie, spar, boast, threaten, justify, signify, concede, plead, and yield. They slap down dominoes, form fists, smooth hair just so. They read, listen to the radio, watch TV, stay in tune.

All this motion and commotion has survival value as part of shaping a mode for doing time. Men already resolved to make the best of what is get right into "jailing," angling for advantage in this world, hammering out lines of power, "calling their best shots," and trying to back them up.

Some men shine shoes, sweep floors, remake beds—straighten things out, get things done. Others, unable to accept the chasm between themselves and those outside, spend long hours composing letters and waiting for mail call. They construct picture frames from pleated cigarette packages to display censored photos of their families, advancing the assertion that there was and will be another place and time. And some few inmates exchange legal notes with the dream of beating the man at his own game.

Several prisoners sleep both day and night, perhaps hoping to wake only when their time is over. But Frank, though on his bunk, has his eyes open and stares at the ceiling, not unconscious, but making no effort to place himself in context and so protect himself.

Alone as he is, Frank nevertheless is not neutral. For instance, his shoes are on his feet and his feet are on the bed. The day guard notices this infraction when he passes, tries to engage Frank's eyes, can't, and walks on, feeling slighted. Already he has given the men fair warning: "Treat me like a prick and I'll fuck you." If Frank is aware that he is jeopardizing himself by offending the guard, he gives no sign, he simply acknowledges nothing but that stretch of ceiling.

In addition to having his shoes on the bed, Frank rumples his bedding as he lies on it. Though not a violation of the letter of the law concerning upkeep of a prisoner's space, what Frank does to his bed is, by the spirit of those rules, at least a misdemeanor. The inmates who try to sleep away their time understand this unwritten standard perfectly, and manage to leave no more than a faint imprint on the blanket as they sleep, as if they hovered over the bed. They do this as easily as they remember, even while in a dream that carries them out through the walls, to keep an arm exposed over the blanket to save the guard from having to shake their beds to see if they've really escaped.

Could the prisoners but join the trusties who clean the warden's house, they would see that he's a tidy man: in his garbage pails no garbage, in his wastebaskets no waste. Frank hasn't earned the privilege of working there, but he has seen how other inmates comport themselves. Though no defiance can be discerned in his posture or stare, he manifests no pride in his quarters. Nor does he look after himself. Shirt wrinkled, hair awry, face covered with acne—well, compared to other prisoners, he's a slob.

The lowriders, gunsels, and would-be torpedoes wear perfect "bonaroos"—starched shirts and "cadillac" pants with wide legs, creases just so, huge cuffs obscuring well-shined shoes, bandanna handkerchief protruding from a back pocket. Hair well greased and slicked straight back, they are clean-shaven except perhaps for a pachuco tuft below the nether lip. Their consorts, the queens, match this display with tight pants, plucked brows, tinted hair, snow-white sneakers, and buttons in lieu of zippers. Christ, even the lames, ducks, and rumpkins know how to dress. But there Frank is. Sallow as the men in from county jail who have yet to acquire the sheen bestowed by three squares and nowhere to go.

Few men here are so unconcerned with appearance. Forever preening before the mirror, shaving carefully, picking over themselves for possible blemishes, endlessly applying lotions and creams, most prisoners strive for a physical beauty to lift them clear of the tawdriness of this life, a beauty to warrant their beings, in spite of their being here.

The unwritten equation goes something like: "I care for my own appearance, therefore I make myself beautiful, hence, though there are no others here to say so, I am worthy of being cared for by others, were they only here to see how I value myself and how beautiful I am."

If Frank's failure to practice this narcissism makes him pariah, so does his use of his bunk. To lie on it to stare into space, thinking? Surely there are all different ways to do time, you can hustle it off, fight, walk, or talk it off, but you don't have to go looking to face it alone. Thinking won't open the front gate.

Given Frank's idiosyncrasies, the question arises as to the nature of his "game." Here it is axiomatic that no one presents himself as he really is. Nearly every prisoner sees himself and others as forever trying to pull something off. And with so many thwarted hungers, it comes as no surprise that selflessness and straightforwardness are also in short supply. There is candor only in the assumption that every last guard and inmate must to some degree be "shined on"—humored, fooled, used, distanced, handled.

The boundaries of most games are time-tested, the formulae pretty clear. Generally, then, the question of interest is whether or not a man is playing what is the right game for him. At first it appears that Frank is just another crazy. One man in the unit, for example, spends most of his time in a chair near the door. Staring after each prisoner who passes, never shifting his weight, he rotates his head as far as it will go, and then brings it back around. "Lighthouse," they call him.

Though he is small—and therefore easy prey—he is left alone because he is crazy, or, as men here see it, because he plays the role of being crazy hard enough to earn its rewards. No one wants the bother, they say, though a homosexual whore is valuable property. No one wants to risk what Lighthouse might do, since his behavior within the boundaries of the crazy game cannot be controlled.

Perhaps also Lighthouse smells of death. To the degree that intentionality is imputed to all action, the general understanding is that a man plays crazy to protect himself, but of course any game can be run too hard, and then one becomes the game.

Whatever the dangers, if indeed he has the freedom of choice, Lighthouse is safe not only because his actions are unpredictable, but because he inspires a fear of contamination. Prisoners avoid contact with him lest they jeopardize the illusion of normality they struggle so hard to maintain. In truth, though, no one is safe here, and the burden of such precariousness reduces sanity to the capacity to treat madness as normal. Even so, not being manifestly crazy assumes great importance. Being like Lighthouse is too explicit a break with all one remembers himself as and hopes again to be.

So it is that no one gets too close to Lighthouse. As a tactic the crazy game works well. Lighthouse is pretty smart for a crazy man, very safe given his size and the hungers of this world. But then he has to live his game. Time will tell.

Frank, however, while aberrant, is not yet more than strange and alone, nor does he seem to be fashioning a new variant of the crazy game. He is simply removed from the flow of prison life. No one bothers, yet, to make him join the fold.

It is during a compulsory lecture for new prisoners that Frank defines himself further. The Captain is laying down the rules, and, in the course of his recital, explains that he will assign every man a job. Though the Captain, toothpick and cigarette working simultaneously, can hardly be called a liberal, prison reforms are generally acceptable to him, particularly as they are implemented.

Every prisoner should be spared the misery of enforced idleness. The Captain swallows this pill happily. Cheap inmate labor yields prison industry profits, which in turn justify salary increases for prison staff. Similarly, though the Captain understands that inmates prefer almost anything which occupies them to the killing monotony of empty days, having them work accords with his philosophy of life. He himself is living testimony to the gospel that a steady job guarantees an early pension.

Whatever his beliefs, the Captain feels no need to explain anything to anyone. Civilians listen with awe to his horror stories about prisoners. "Custody knows best," he likes to say, and he labels himself a "progressive" for having suggested that efficiency would increase if attack dogs were stationed between the double fences.

The Captain never ventures into abstraction with his fellow employees, and has been conditioned to expect that inmates agree with him, have no opinions, or know enough to bite their tongues. In his exegesis of prison policy, then, he settles for rote phrase with the ease of a man long used to *fait accompli*: "All prisoners will be assigned a job detail."

The Captain is just switching to another track when he notices a hand raised before him. Though aware that only snitches and incompetents ask questions, the Captain is flattered. If the prisoner has become a pupil, then his guard must be a teacher.

"Why do we have to work?" Frank asks. Nonplussed, immediately irritated with himself for falling into what he is sure must have been a trap, the Captain replies: "Every man here works."

Apparently missing the finality of this response, and before the Captain can begin to reorganize his thoughts, Frank says, "I understand that, Captain, but why?" Angry now, resolved to get Frank's name and number though his questions showed no overt malice, the Captain spells it out: "Every man works because, one, it's in the book, that's why, and because, two, we follow the book, that's why." Sure that the subject is closed, having been forced to explicate his metaphysic to a mere prisoner, the Captain is without defense when Frank presses on. "But why is it in the book?"

For several long moments after this last question the orientation room is absolutely still. And then, across the void of the silence, speaking for a need the Captain could not begin to imagine, Frank takes another, and larger, step. "I can occupy myself," he says.

Now the Captain is no longer flustered. What was almost a venture into ontology is safely back in the realm of crime and punishment. Telling Frank to see him after the lecture, the Captain is once more in charge. As he regains his pace his words carry themselves to completion.

Days pass and no one learns more about Frank, in part

because the Captain sends him to the hole for refusing to work. But even when Frank appears on the yard one day, wearing the dark overalls of men assigned to the furniture factory, he keeps to himself. Unlike most prisoners, Frank shows little need to bolster the paltriness of his life inside with stories of exploits on the streets. Yet prison is if nothing else a leveler, and in time he finds a niche as a regular on the basketball court, trying vainly to outrun and outshoot the Indians. He makes a team and some friends, and his story filters out.

Apparently he was living quietly in Los Angeles, smoking some dope, selling a little, doing a lot of nothing, so near to being broke that he had to sell his car. Bored, he began using downers, which only left him depressed. Out window-shopping one morning, seeing a shirt he wanted, he emptied his pockets and found that he was down to his last twenty dollars. The shirt cost twenty-three. His depression deepened.

Still walking around downtown Los Angeles, he passed a used-car lot and noticed a car with the keys in the ignition. Before thought came action: he hopped in and drove off. He went several miles before the adrenalin rush subsided enough for him to see that the car was a 1960 Rambler, worth almost nothing but the felony.

Spirits understandably lower, he drove around town wondering what to do. Finally, passing a bank, he decided that what he needed was some money. Pulling in at the curb, parking the car, he walked inside, stood waiting in line, and, when his turn came, told the cashier to give him some money. As he ran out to the street to make his getaway he stuffed the bills into his pockets.

At curbside, however, the Rambler was now wedged between two other parked cars. Frank jumped in and wrestled with the wheel, but of course there was no power steering. Sweating bullets, he was just edging out of the space when he heard the classic "Stop or I'll shoot!"

He pressed the accelerator to the floor, but the small engine could not absorb the gas, and the Rambler sputtered slowly down the street as shots riddled the windows and mirror. One cartridge shattered Frank's elbow. When the car finally gathered speed, he had time to notice that his favorite white pants were now bloody.

Reaching his neighborhood without further trouble, he abandoned the car and, still bleeding, walked through a playground to his apartment. Staggering upstairs and in the door, he sat down at the kitchen table, emptied his pockets to count the money, and fell to the floor unconscious.

His landlady, who lived below, heard the crash. Never one to personally intrude on the privacy of her tenants, she called the police emergency service. When Frank regained consciousness he was in the hospital unit of the Los Angeles County Jail. By the time his head began to clear he carried two felony convictions, eight years of time, and had lost twenty dollars for his day's work. As the bank later stated, in response to his letter (he wanted the twenty dollars to spend at the commissary), all the money recovered from the robbery came from a pile of bills on his kitchen table. They assumed the money was theirs, and in any case felt no obligation to honor his claim.

As Frank's story get around it changes little. A bigger step is that he has formed affiliations. Whatever his game is, he can be pegged accurately enough by the company he keeps. Given his friendships, his explanation that he wanted some time to figure out what really happened that day, why it happened, that he went to solitary to do so, that even there he found no answer and so finally said he was ready to work, none of this matters in any primary way except to him.

With the passage of time, on rare occasions when he is at ease with fellow sufferers, Frank can sometimes be persuaded to recount the events of that memorable day. Though his friends laugh at his wan smile, though they claim to understand what they did wrong, who did them wrong, they are of course on the yard with him to hear the story told. And whatever they make of their own falls, whatever they think they won or lost, they too walk off their time, day for day, one day at a time.

಼ೕ

Out on the asphalt basketball court, when Willie again uses muscle and finesse to wrestle a rebound right out of his hands, Jackson evens things up by smashing Willie's jaw. Of course he waits to do so until Willie is looking the other way, suspecting nothing. But who said it was just a game?

Over on the nearby baseball diamond, two sets of all-stars play as though they represented eighteen different clubs. Hurly, who is not alone in thinking himself big-league material, taunts the pitcher, dancing back and forth with too long a lead off first base. When the batter drives one deep into center, Hurly sprints for second, slows to see the outfielder bobble the ball, and races for third. He knows he's lookin' good, hell, he's a one-man team.

Though clearly the throw from center field will be late and wide, Hurly approaches the bag with a fancy hook slide. As the dust settles he can be seen writhing on the ground, foot hanging from leg at a crazy angle. Broken ankle. Call the guard.

Prisoners not still watching the fight on the basketball court drift on over toward third base. Just before Hurly passes out from the pain he begins to scream. Hearing him, one prisoner in the crowd walks over to where he lies. "Hey, fuckhead," he says, "shut your fuckin' hole."

Minutes pass, and finally the stretcher crew arrives. The prisoner rejoins his friends, and they stand watching as Hurly is carried off the yard toward the hospital. "Fuckin' showboat," the prisoner says, "thought he was superjock. Shit. Dumb turd. What goes around comes around."

૩☙

Two-thirty in the morning, not a sound from the cell-block, and in the tiny office at the door to the main corridor, under the overhead bulb, the guard the prisoners call Absurdo leans back in the swivel chair engrossed in a copy of *Outdoor Life*. Without looking away from the magazine, he guides his hand past the shards of a sandwich, finds his cup and brings it to his lips, gulps down its contents, belches, and, sighing, puts down both cup and magazine. Getting up with a yawn, he stretches, adjusts the belt below his large belly, hitches up his pants, and heads out into the empty block, flashlight in hand.

Following the mandatory procedure for night counts, he walks past all one hundred and twenty cells—three tiers on each side of the block, twenty cells to a tier—shining his light through the small panes on each metal door. A squat and solitary figure in the blue fluorescence, he punctuates his passage through the darkened block with one hundred and twenty white shots from his flashlight.

The squeak of his rubber-soled shoes, the jangle of his keys, and his own labored breathing are loud in his ears, the only sounds he hears. As he finishes the count he descends the stairs, and, coming to a stop, looks once more around the block. Still empty. Suddenly aware of the low hum of the night lights over the beat of his pulse, he has the feeling of movement, as though the cellblock were a ship advancing through the darkness, some vessel far larger than the human cargo it contains.

Though he likes company and would prefer not to work the lonely graveyard shift, Absurdo comes on duty two hours after the prisoners are locked in for the night. Nor has he any contact with other staff, save for hourly phone checks with the guard in "Control." Alone in the stillness, he sees no one except the sleeping figures glimpsed as he does the counts. If he moves slowly, he can hear muffled snores and groans from within the cells, and occasionally he can even make out the words when a prisoner talks in his sleep. "The inside sure looks smaller than the outside," mutters one man in a fevered dream.

Only an emergency breaks Absurdo's isolation. One night an old black prisoner has an epileptic fit. Hurrying to unlock the cell, Absurdo picks the small man up, carrying him down from the tier, out through the block, and on along the endless main corridor to the prison hospital. Head tossing, mouth foaming, beyond all control, the poor creature shakes with terror before falling unconscious in Absurdo's arms.

Emergencies are rare, however, and normally by the time dawn comes Absurdo is starved for company. As the night lights, controlled by some central rheostat, switch off, he hears the early risers sweeping floors and making beds. While they prepare for the start of their day Absurdo points to the end of his own. Though he knows he has the night watch because he's on the Captain's shit list (guilty of lenience to prisoners and a sloppy appearance), still it feels like some kind of victory to be heading home as the Captain passes into the institution to begin work.

Absurdo watches the clock in his office. One last click, and the morning buzzer sounds in the darkness, wrenching from their dreams those for whom waking means moving with open eyes through routines a somnambulist could perform, until at last day is done and the dreams with closed eyes begin once more. As in breeding caves for chickens, lights switch on, lights switch off, natural functions take place, matter is transmuted from one form to another. There are these rhythms, there is this life.

Absurdo feels for the men. Intuitively he understands that he could be in their place, but is not threatened by the thought. Moreover, the prisoners' common taunt—that the guards are themselves doing time, twenty-year sentences waiting for that pension—is of course true. Absurdo hasn't had much freedom, no time to explore, just school, the service, marriage, children, and the first government job that required nothing more than a high-school diploma. Two weeks off a year, three after another five on the job, Absurdo knows about being institutionalized, he knows about time.

He moves through the empty block. Shaving beard heavy, uniform rumpled and food-stained, shoes scuffed and tie off to the side, in no way measuring up to the warden's military standard, looking more like an exhausted bus driver, he heads for the stairs with a last cup of coffee.

From one of the tiers above, a prisoner eager for chow calls through the small glassless window of his cell door, "O.K., Absurdo, open 'em up, rack." Absurdo smiles. Then another voice sings out, "Hey, Absurdo, you fat son of a bitch, rack these fuckin' ranges." He smiles again. He likes the men, is glad they're awake, and has even come to think of himself by the nickname they've given him. Genial, moved by lethargic good will where taut fear prevails, short, fat, and sloppy, he is truly without pretension, comic, even absurd.

Though the men value him because he has so little need for the armor of his role, and though he is never

ambitious at their expense (and so without hope for pro-
motion), still between Absurdo and the prisoners there
is one serious conflict of interest: Absurdo hates to
"rack"—to open the cells. Nothing bothers him more
than to have once again to climb the six tiers of the cell-
block to six separate times unlock and lock the ranges of
cells.

The prisoners, of course, want all the freedom of movement that regulations permit, and only a guard can open
the cells. To be locked in when it is time for chow, for
instance, is at first irritating and then too clear a re-
minder of the restraints all around. The men are drawn
to Absurdo, they would never let anyone harm him, but
still, there is the question of racking.

"Come on, Absurdo, you tub of guts, rack these
ranges."

"In a moment, gentlemen," he replies, "just don't
leave without me."

"Come on, scumbag, shake your fat ass."

Absurdo moves heavily up the stairs toward the third
tier.

"You heard the man, Absurdo, you got to rack 'em
sometime."

"Like hell I do," he replies.

"Rack 'em, damn it, it's in the Bill of Rights."

"Fuck the Bill of Rights, I got a union."

"Screw your union and your mama too."

"Sure as hell you won't be doin' nothin' to her, not
for five more big ones, will you, sucker?"

"Jesus Christ, Absurdo, give us a break, will ya?"

By now Absurdo has reached the top tier. Unlocking

the iron casing with his master key, grunting as he pulls the two heavy sections apart, pressing the lever that releases the double night locks, he turns the wheel by its handle and watches the twenty steel doors slide back on their runners. In the instant the doors open twenty men pop out of their cells and move for the stairs and chow. Peering down the range like an engineer checking the track, waiting for one last moment to make sure that everyone is out who wants out, Absurdo turns the wheel back, slams the casing shut, and locks it.

In the growing din, as men shout to each other with the start of their day, as they either savor the relative freedom of being out of their cells or rue the loss of privacy and protection, as all the pleasures and pressures of prison life are once more upon them, Absurdo—already bobbing in a sea of bantering inmates—heads on down to the next tier to rack 'em again.

ॐ

Deacon is curious about LSD. "What's that shit like anyway, man?" He's about six feet seven, two hundred and fifty pounds, black, with a smile that just won't quit. *Psychedelic*, as they say.

"Well, think of it this way, Deacon. Suppose for a minute that this place isn't real, that you've imagined it, or, even better, suppose that just now as we walk and talk you're at the tail end of a dream. You with me?

"So none of this is really happening—those aren't real cells over there, those aren't real guards, and we aren't really having this conversation. It's all part of your dream. Right now, right this minute, you're really on those silk sheets back in your pad, and you're tossing and turning, having a bad dream that seems incredibly real. And the bad dream you're having is that you're in prison, that you've been doing lots of time, too much time, and that at this particular point of doing time you're having a conversation with some dude about LSD and it's making you uneasy and in a minute you're going to cut him loose and head on down to chow.

"But of course you are really just finally fighting your way out of the end of your nightmare. Any moment now you'll snap out of those silk sheets sweating like a dog, your ol' lady hanging all over you. 'What's the matter, baby,' she'll say, 'take it easy, baby, everything's gonna be all right.'

"You'll blink your eyes hard, shake your head to clear it, and then start to tell her about that dream you were just dreaming. Of course she'll hold you close, tell you sweet things, but you'll be wondering. You'll still be thinking about that dream, how real it felt, how just as you woke up you were talking to that dude in prison, and how before you went to chow the last thing he said was: 'And it is the not knowing which of the two worlds is real that is at least part of what LSD is about, if you see what I mean.' "

Deacon shakes his head. "That's some heavy shit, Thomas." Too heavy, really. It doesn't do, doesn't do at all, to get into this kind of talk, it breeds anxieties one is ashamed to feel. Strange, to be unsettled by contradiction, to be disturbed by just the kind of ambiguity that

49

might have pleased the mind on the streets, but here metaphor is too subtle, paradox not only elusive but actually threatening. Dangers abounding, it pays to keep things linear. Guards and inmates alike enforce a code that both censors feeling and checks expression of emotion. Here to voice sadness is to "snivel," and to persist is to "hold," to hold on for dear life.

Given the discomfort my words have brought, then, it's a pleasure to read Deacon's mail to him. To our great relief the familiar language of the letter reminds us where we stand, cuing appropriate response.

HONEY,

How are you feeling today? Hope they arent trateing you too bad down there. Sorry Hon but my back is hurting liek hell. Hon I am going to try and get some money to rent a place to live. While you are in jaile. Hon when is your new trail going to be and what time will it end? Do you want me to bring some clean paints and things for you.

Sweetheart, did the cops give you a rough time? Love, I am going to go home for a while to see my Grandparents for 5 or 6 days. Hon do you care if I go? Deacon please go to the Doctor will you Hon will you go? Hon will you do this for me It will be the only time I've ask you to. (please) Love, when you come home out jale you are going to beat my ass in. Baby I miss you more than anyone hear could know. I hope you get some fat on your body. I am going to try to gain some pounds. . . .

Deacon smiles when I finish reading, he's glad to have forgotten about LSD, relieved to be clear about what world he's in. Simpler just to do the time, particularly with his woman waitin' home, saying she's waiting. It's one way to do time, this ritual exchange between inside and out, it makes the time pass just to work through the formulae. Grief, despair, anger, penitence, hope, loneliness, they hang in the prison air ready to once more be molded into the litanies of being down. "You know I'm going straight, baby". "Going to get me a job"; "When I get out, honey, you'll see"; "I know it's hard on you too"; "Have you seen that lawyer for me, baby"; "That two-timing motherfucker"; "Since you left me, baby"; "Have mercy"; "Ain't it hard."

Deacon is still smiling, he's really pleased to hear from her. The dialogue goes on: his complaint, her concern, his lament, her betrayal, their reconciliation, their separation, whatever it is and will be until he's back on the block, back to his silk sheets and Cadillac and runnin' round. Round and round. Unless he doesn't make it out.

As Deacon heads to chow, anxiety about the nature of reality quickly subsides. What remains is the struggle to hold on to an awareness of our loneliness and loss, lest even that understanding be denied us. But relentlessly petty needs concretize our concerns, and we are too willingly numbed. If to feel is to feel bad, who needs it?

Though the timeless rhythms of the formulae for doing time impel one to accept the terms of this life, such continuity with the past occasionally creates anomalies which force feeling alive once more. I think of Deacon on the prison farm, driving the tractor, baling hay. Toting the bales. Surely forms persist, prison is after all a state-maintained anachronism, but there he is, a genial giant, straw hat on his head, bandanna round his neck, towering over the white guards. And doing the same chores that black men have performed for white overseers for the last three hundred and fifty years.

If Deacon is aware of his place in this continuum, he doesn't let on. As much as the guards, he avoids like the plague anything resembling ideology. Or perhaps it is just simple truth that is avoided. Clearly, were he moved to anger Deacon could easily snap the spines of the three guards. If he begins to let that kind of feeling speak in himself, however, those silk sheets will be no more than something he once dreamed he dreamed. To see the day that his memories are the stuff of real life, Deacon shuns the Muslims, he does his own time, garners what pleasure he can from the work itself, and above all trusts that the real world corresponds to his reveries, that those fine women really are out there, and waiting for him.

For their part, the guards fully appreciate Deacon's compliance with traditional modes. The big fella certainly can do a day's labor. Even so, it's hard not to want something more from him. But he already works so hard. What else can he do? Well, maybe he can sing. "Oh the Deacon went down"? Or perhaps:

> If I had the Man like the Man had me,
> Wake up in the mornin', I'd set him free.

೭‌ಎ

Though it is already an hour after final lockup, we find ourselves released from our cells to watch TV, and, dazed, we walk down from the tiers. Tonight, we learn, Americans are to set foot on the moon.

Momentous as the landing is, we here are struck more by this break in our routine. So immutable are the prison's rhythms that we wonder what, really, is happening. Perhaps, comes the suggestion, the warden is moved by the moon landing, and wants us to share his feelings. "No way," Dicky says. "If the warden saw the Virgin he wouldn't know whether to shit or go blind." Maybe, we decide, the warden is matching the astronaut's efforts and doing the impossible—altering the pace of our lives.

Though the schedule change makes for a giddy holiday atmosphere, some men look anxiously to their cells, wedded to private timetables. The personal pulse matches, anticipates, and so protects against submission to the institution's relentless routine. Not only is this concentric inner circle of regulation best left unbroken, but the evening's excitement carries with it the risk of insomnia, and so more waking time to do.

We sit watching the screen, for once no one preparing to crush a skull to enforce a preference. On no matter which station we see simulations of the rocket in flight. Where the capsule spins, how, why, to what end. There are, voice of America explains, human beings on the moon, Americans, and an American flag.

So bad is the televised image that I cannot but believe it is real. My hope that the project abort (nothing personal against the astronauts) is ludicrous. Why identify going to the moon with the government itself? Yet this success not only launches a new dream for the species, but, simultaneously, renders my fixed universe relatively smaller. And who am I, in this new and larger human realm, my concerns so diminutized, to dare struggle with forces that can carry off such a feat?

The moon landing has yet another impact on life here. The glare of the guard lights on the wall is so strong that only the moon is bright enough to be seen in the night sky. Until tonight it was free, well beyond our lives, we could follow its changes, and through it transcend our limits here below. Though stars hold so much more possibility, it was the moon alone which was beyond man's reach and still visible to us. Now man is there, the Man, of all men to have made it.

"It's a man's world," Dicky says. Indeed it is. No women here. And if God made the firmament, it had to be man to construct this concrete tomb for the living. Man who, from nothing, would build an environment ruling out the first five days of Creation.

Even as *Homo sapiens* extends his influence in the solar system, I decide to abandon the moon. Why not find transcendence in what is sure to remain, in the sheer stuff of our thwarted lives. God knows there's plenty to marvel at here.

"Chump," Dicky says to Al.

"Look who's talkin'," Al replies.

It's Dicky talking, Dicky who spent one too many afternoons drinking wine and snorting coke, Dicky who finally put his infallible bank robbery plan into action. In the moment itself, when the teller turned to check something on the computer, Dicky reached over the counter and cleaned out the till. Withdrawing the hand which held the money, turning to go, his eyes met the eyes of a black teller in an adjoining booth who was staring right at him. "That's cool," Dicky said to himself, and settled the possible threat by giving the brother a power salute. Talk about the mystery of life! It never occurred to the black teller to slow the progress of his foot to the alarm button on the floor.

Back on television they're making no mistakes. Winners up there, losers down below? It tests your convictions, living right in man's world, nothing above. Jesus Christ Almighty, it could even make a man religious.

Richard orbits the track behind the Indians, lap after lap, his lope always the same, steady and effortless. Eyes squinting in the sun, he smiles each time he glides by. Sleepy in the heat, we chart his transit through endless turns. Barring impediments he could run forever.

The Indians run as though their heritage demanded it, as though they carried genes which must be fed so many laps per week. They run without expression, perhaps to mask their knowledge that one day the centrifugal force they gather rounding the corners—that momentum and a desperation they can no longer check—will carry them off the track, over to the edge of the yard, and up the first of the double fences. There to be picked off by the tower guard and his rifle with the telescopic sight even before their hands are bloodied by the barbed wire.

Richard is the only non-Indian who can keep up with them. The blacks run fast, but only for sprints; they have no use for distance. Few whites run at all. Only Richard stays with the Indians, gliding just behind them as they impassively drive onward.

The Indians never speak to Richard. Possibly they believe him to be without serious concerns. Indeed, child-like in his directness, Richard seems more than satisfied with yet another fine day in the sun. Though he is clearly *compos mentis*—clowning to ease tensions, for instance, when trouble threatens—prisoners believe him to be a simpleton. The guards, concurring, think he's crazy to run barefoot on the cinder track. Saying he can ruin his feet if he wants to, they allow him to break the rules.

Because Richard has neither money on the books nor visitors to smuggle him dope, few men cultivate his friendship. In terms of what is vital to power inside he has little to offer. At the same time he is genuinely affable, and so obviously without privilege that no one can envy him. Safe, then, just barely, but without a hustle, Richard stays on the yard in the sun, running.

Strange, that no one attributes any nuance to him. Though he appears incapable of deceit, it violates the most basic tenet of this life to take him at face value. Surely even Richard has some private place where he is free of the mask survival requires. Nevertheless, Richard is held to be no more than he seems. Harmless, a lame, a stoned acid eater who is too spaced out to mind doing time.

If the inmates, appraising him, find Richard only of no practical value, the guards have a real stake in believing him to be a fool. Trapped in prison waiting for pensions, saved and suffocated by the Civil Service, reading about dope and orgies during endless time-clock hours, they have in Richard a real hippy, and are all too willing to believe that his mind is blown, that he could care less where he finds himself. In this, however, like the inmates, they are wrong. Richard's thoughts are collected, he does not like prison. And, once, he planned an escape.

True, many men dream of breaking out. But fantasies aside, attempts are few and far between. Apart from the penalties of failure (an additional sentence and loss of good time), parole always dangles just beyond reach, an incentive to wait only a little longer. And ultimately time logged within the walls becomes an investment in the completion of the sentence, a down payment it seems imprudent to forfeit.

Most escape attempts are made by short-timers working outside the wall during the last weeks of their sentences. Nothing to look forward to in the free world, some men earn the right to stay here by running only several hundred yards.

Other prisoners working outside break under the tension of the last few days of waiting. Cars pass, children play, and these first signs of a life beyond prison trigger the fear that freedom may never again come so close. Unable to trust any longer that the gates will open on the appointed day, that so enforced a contract will be honored, some prisoners take off.

Occasionally men saw through cell bars, cut holes in the double fences, and make it. But without money, few friends to trust, they are picked up stealing a car or breaking into a house. Or, unable to stay away, nowhere else to go, they head home and are apprehended.

In his own case Richard understood all this, but he had a plan, and good reason to try it. After several sessions with the parole board, having watched his crime partner depart long since, Richard came to the conclusion that he just wasn't slick enough to earn a parole. He didn't understand how to run a game.

More important, he had had enough. In fact he was a hippy, busted in San Francisco for possession of several pounds of weed. He had tried to get behind his time, seen no reason why prison couldn't be a positive, even religious, experience, but in time he was just worn out with the death trip, Yoga and meditation notwithstanding. Assigned to the greenhouse outside the wall to cultivate plants for the warden's office, he developed his plan.

The way he figured it, the mountains were only sixty or seventy miles away. If he could reach them, running, it would be no trouble at all to head right up the range, on foot, fifty miles a day, finally reaching the sanctuary of Big Sur. There he'd be just another stoned freak.

For weeks he worked on a survival pouch, stashing medication and matches, sewing special warm shirts. Because he wanted the run to be really organic, he took pains to search for proper food, but had trouble locating anything except pork to store away. Finally, however, he was ready to go. He even had two tablets of LSD for the trip.

They didn't find him until nightfall of the day he set out. In part it took them that long because they assumed he had simply fallen asleep in the grass near the greenhouse. It was already early evening when they saw him sitting in lotus posture at the foot of a hackberry tree less than two miles from the walls. He must have needed no more than several minutes to run that far. And even after they found him they had no inkling of his plan, only remarking on the strange sack of unguents, seeds, and flowers in the grass nearby.

Apparently Richard answered no questions. Even as they surrounded him, guns cocked, lanterns held high, dogs straining at the leads, he simply sat there chanting mantras. Having decided to take the acid as he left, he felt its rush and eased into his stride. Arms loose, hands relaxed, lungs rich with oxygen, head absolutely clear. As he surged forward all bars were as if they had never been, cells and walls even less than a bad dream. Gliding into his true rhythms, cleansed of all sadness, he realized he was home. Tears of exultation in his eyes, he sang out one long cry of wonder, he bore witness to the lizard's orange tongue and the blackbird's red wing, and then, thus amazed, he sat down to celebrate and to give thanks.

ॐ

It takes time to learn the pace here. What's jailhouse wisdom on the subject? "Walk slow, drink a lot of water, and keep your hands out of your pockets."

Walk slow? It's true, often I automatically break into a trot as I head for the yard. To play some ball. This has nothing to do with prison, and my system gears up to enthusiasm. But even when a guard doesn't frown me down—"Running only on the track"—I notice that no one else moves at my speed.

This absence of visible energy and exuberance startles the eye. Fifteen hundred men under age thirty walking with measured steps? Clearly, as with midgets and mutants, something is out of phase. Possessed of youthful vigor but prematurely aware that it does not suffice, callow but subtle in the ways of survival, the inmates are hybrids in life's garden, healthy growth onto which has been grafted knowledge that should come later, if ever.

Walk slow. They talk about "running" a game, but the verb must have nothing to do with velocity. Yet despite the pace, camouflaged by it, there are passions in this hothouse life. Sleepy, for instance, isn't just slow. He's only waiting, with those heavy eyelids, waiting to strike. He'll "drive on" someone, bend someone to his will, not fast, no, but inexorably. What's the hurry? Where can they run to? He'll fuck 'em, fuck 'em around, fuck 'em up.

One might initially be surprised that there can be sex here at all, whatever the component of violence. But helplessness need not, apparently, be synonymous with impotence. Even so, how explain the hardening of our penises when we weaken in so many other ways?

Working through this question with me, inmate casuists are quick to point out that as we live at the sufferance of the guards, so free men live at the whim of the gods. Free men have erections. As with the greater, so with the lesser. *Quod erat demonstrandum.*

If like free men we have erections, our sex is a grotesque exaggeration of the worst abuses outside. Angry and stigmatized, afraid and ashamed of our fears, we desperately need others to abase themselves to elevate us, if only by comparison.

Here, to put a man in a subordinate sexual role is to fuck him in the ass, to "turn him out," turn him inside out. If a man fights he can usually stave off an assault. But if he cannot fight and keep fighting, then in prison terms he deserves what he gets. Sure that women get fucked and that men do the fucking, would-be rapists will release their prey only if the struggle is in itself enough to confirm their manhood.

Here the men pressured or beaten into being "women" define the possibilities of sexual contact: homosexuality means defeat because it is grounded on rape. And worse, homosexuality here is abetted by officials who—having barred all contact with women—then treat us like the animals we show ourselves to be. So this is what we were sentenced to by desiccated judges whose remaining passions are authority, abstraction, and order. We are consigned to keepers who, for miserable stipends, either keep us celibate or encourage us as we humiliate each other.

And those who choose to be "women"? The desire to be cared for and to care for others gets played out at its lowest possible level, reduced to the willingness to accept abuse to at least be noticed and be spared the fear of something worse. Bought and sold, one of the currencies of this life, these "women" are whores and slaves, sure of their station, easy in the peace of those who cannot lose themselves because they are already lost.

Sex is everywhere here, all the time, fifteen hundred penises, almost as many inventive minds. I sit on the second tier surveying the cellblock below, and Rio passes by. Tall, lithe, reputed to have had estrogen shots on the streets, specially embroidered pants outlining a firm rump and what must surely be a vagina, Rio today received a miniskirt from Smokey, a little something he had made over in the leather factory. Smokey, a real lover, would think nothing of killing someone for not referring to "her" as "she."

As I watch Rio sashay toward her cell, Tex comes over. "Look at that," he says, watching her disappear. "Sheuuut. She makes my dick hard as chinese 'rithmetic." Pondering the unattainable for a long moment, he finally snaps himself back to what's at hand. "Say, home," he says, "do me a favor? I'm gonna get my knob polished. Look out for the Man?" Giving me a big grin, towel over his arm and toilet kit in hand, Tex steps on down to the mop room. A "homosexual" darts in after him and pulls the door shut.

Even as I watch over them and the mop-room light is extinguished, Martinez comes down the stairs from the third-floor shower. It's a touchy moment as he sees me see him leave this popular trysting spot. "Hey, Thomas," he says, when he reaches my perch, "you don't think I'm no queer or nothin'?" "Not at all, man," I reply, "not at all. I know you, just 'cause you get up there and some dude sucks your dick, I know you're no queer."

Lucky for me Martinez is a stranger to irony. He likes my answer, he's been wondering himself. He knows what they say: "Start out pitchin', end up catchin'."

Tex is still at it when Stan comes by with his contraband pornography collection. I can have it for the night, free. Though Stan's generous, I decline. The shots are still too raw for my taste. Maybe in another six months.

Below on the flats a pretty slight boy heads for his cell. Were the homosexuality here a shade less brutal I'd want him for myself. When the boy first arrived we explained that he would have to fight to save himself. One night a lowrider named Max pinned him in the shower room, but a guard approached so he cut the boy loose. I spoke with Max. "He's pussy," Max said. "You want him, we can work that out, but otherwise, I'm telling you he's pussy and he's mine." We argued, but I was out of line. Max would do no more than give the boy the chance he already had, the chance to fight.

We offered the boy a weapon, tried to show him something about taking a punch. Hell, he might even surprise Max, we told him, turn *him* out. But the boy found nothing to smile at. He was terrified of physical pain, and for sure pain was coming his way soon, one way or another.

In the shower room several nights later, when Max drove on him, the boy picked up a chair and tried to shield himself. Max ripped the chair away, took a bar of soap in his fist, knocked the boy across the face with the back of his hand, smeared some soap on his penis, and entered the boy from behind as the boy lay sprawled face down on the shower-room floor.

ह‍‌

Once a week, twice on holiday weekends, films are shown in the auditorium. Clustered by race, only the homosexual mating ground ("Vaseline Alley") integrated, two shifts of seven hundred prisoners watch movies projected onto two large sheets fastened together with safety pins.

Beyond the stimulation images of any outside world provide, movies mean release because while watching them prisoners are safe from "arrest." Like the chow hall and the yard, where with so many men together a riot is always possible, the auditorium is *de facto* a free zone. Thwarted, but sensible enough to overlook those offenses they can see, the guards stay back at the rear doors of the theater. Inside, shouting inmates stuff themselves with commissary candy hoarded for the show, and use the cover of near darkness to have sex and get high.

Nearly every week the feature is preceded by a Roadrunner cartoon. Year in and year out prisoners watch the fox scheme and get outfoxed. Always—beep, beep—he ends up chasing the roadrunner right to the edge of a cliff. And always, as the bird screeches to a halt, the fox shoots past, hangs suspended in thin air suffering the shock of recognition, and then takes his inevitable plunge.

The features run the gamut, but are clearly chosen to stay well within the mainstream of American taste. It is no surprise, then, that most are full of violence. Over and again a lone figure—cowboy, detective, soldier—knocks somebody around, off, or up.

Though criminals generally lose in these epics, prisoners have little trouble identifying with the heroes, since

64

questions of law are usually subordinate to the code of the loner. The vision that animates most men here, practiced fantasts that they are, is the stuff of dreams for the larger culture too: an individual on his own, settling a score his way, everyone else be damned.

Occasionally this unanimity between the gunsel dream of the prisoner and the broader cultural myth breaks down. When *The Green Berets* is shown, most prisoners try initially to side with John Wayne, but even he can't make a Western of the war in Vietnam. Though few inmates are eager to identify with Viet Cong being mauled by gunship fire, Wayne's feeble lines are, none-theless, hooted down.

Men leave the auditorium unsatisfied. At the rear door a fight erupts. A nose is shattered, an eye gouged. As guards wrestle three men off to the hole, prisoners pouring onto the main corridor toward their cellblocks are without question back in the real world.

For their part prison authorities also have troubles with the movies. *One Hundred Rifles*, for example, which in the catalogue seems only another Western, material-izes on the prison screen with Jimmy Brown (a black) coupling with Raquel Welch (a white, though she plays a Mexican). Black prisoners cheer, white prisoners stalk out of the auditorium, and the warden rages even after he learns that Miss Welch kept a towel between Brown and herself during the love scenes.

Selection problems aside, sometimes there are freak accidents. Having approved a special film request by the Catholic chaplain on behalf of Latin inmates, audi-torium overflowing with men of all faiths eager for any diversion, the censors learn only as the titles roll and action begins that the film is not *Carmen* but *Carné*, not opera but pornography. Of course the film must run to completion. To stop it would cause a riot.

Even without such memorable failures, the authorities find it hard to select films which advance our rehabilitation. In *The Thomas Crown Affair*, for example, Steve McQueen plays a wellborn criminal who commits a sensational robbery and then romances the heroine/pursuer. For part of the film he is apparently on the verge of being betrayed. But at the end (with prisoners in the auditorium shouting "Watch out, man, don't trust the bitch!"), he foils her plot, making a successful solitary flight to freedom.

Truly escapist stuff, this film, a prisoner's dream. For weeks men speak of McQueen's class, and, by extension, their own. Months of regret are forgotten, failures reworked into successes that almost were.

One other film inspires us all, but in a very different way. In *Planet of the Apes* Charlton Heston plays a starship commander who emerges from a time warp to land on what seems to be a strange planet. It is strikingly similar to his home Earth, with one important difference: here man is naked, wild, and without language, whereas apes have a civilization and can speak.

Captured by ape horsemen just after he lands, Heston is imprisoned with some of the primitive human beings. Voice lost from a blow to the throat, he struggles in vain to manifest his "higher" qualities. Over and again, his ape keepers regard his efforts to communicate as only the clever mimicry of an inferior creature which happens to resemble them anatomically. In time Heston makes contact, but winning recognition of his true capacities only increases his jeopardy. Committed to orthodox simian theology, which holds that humans are irremediably "animal," the ruling ape scientist is determined to destroy him.

Soon after Heston's capture, as an ape throws him into a cell, a prisoner in the auditorium calls out, "Hey, there's the Captain!" Immediately, amid jeers and laughter, each ape guard is paired with one of ours. As the story progresses, as Heston is reduced to no more than what his keepers believe him to be, the prison audience is increasingly engrossed in the film. The congruities ultimately overwhelm: the apes are our guards, and each of us is Heston.

At the turning point of the film he is still unable to speak. Certain that he will soon be murdered or lobotomized, he decides to escape. Through the haze of cigarette smoke that hangs thick in the auditorium air we see him slip out to the streets and steal through the ape city. The alarm sounds. Ape guards in pursuit, soon he is tracked down, cornered, and brought to bay.

The lassos of the ape guards tighten around his neck, and our jeers are forgotten. As we watch, now silent, he is pulled back and forth, helpless, gasping for breath. Assaulted too long by this terrifying inversion which denies his true nature, driven to an ultimate effort, Heston manages to pull the ropes free from his throat, and finds his voice to cry out: "Take your hands off me, you dirty apes!"

A screenwriter's joy, these words, but hearing them,

long since sharing Heston's torment, we surge to our feet with an enormous roar. Surprised by the depth of our feeling, we applaud, whistle, scream, and stamp our feet. The house lights come on, the screen image fades, more guards line the doorway, but we who so often are pitted against each other, we who so brutally cut each other down, we human beings refuse to stop until we have had enough.

છ≫

Nowhere to run, nowhere to hide. The mind builds its own prisons. In my dream she comes to visit, believing me to be who I was. Love subordinate to need, I try to conceal that I am more than diminished.

In the dream we sit facing each other. She reaches over for a kiss, and in that same instant a guard pulls me from behind. "I told you," he says in my dream, "no physical contact." Her eyes lock on his hand. "Don't let him touch you," they seem to be screaming. "Make him stop, I know you can."

In my letter today I say nothing of the dream. It's my own, and I keep it to myself. Another wrong step.

Trapped, knowing what it is to be trapped, I should insist that there is no obligation. Why should we both live through this? But still, knowing she will not leave me while I'm down, I cannot set her free.

Her letter arrives, and with it a poem she says she wishes she had written:

Since time began
I have waited for you.

For ten thousand days
I have walked out to meet you.

Empires have passed,
Rivers diminished,
Mountains bowed.

But my spirit has grown beyond myself,
Covering the whole world from dusk to
    daybreak.
Wherever you go now,
You walk with me.

ॐ

Clearly force is the tie that binds. Eliminate walls,
gun towers, rifles, and bars, and there'd be rapid depopu-
lation here. But both prisoners and guards tacitly con-
spire to domesticate the raw power that keeps us all
together. Prisoners ward off total helplessness by con-
ceding the outer boundaries, establishing comfort and
controls within these limits. Guards make their violence
primarily procedural, lest they have to fear that each
passing inmate might be the one to deliver a shank to
the belly. Yet though both sides have good reason to
understate the coercion fundamental to this life, such
collective denial suggests that the truth will out.

One Monday afternoon, having repeatedly been

denied four weeks' wages because of persistent bureaucratic error, the hundred men in the furniture factory refuse to return to work until the pay is credited to their
commissary accounts. They move out onto the yard, in
violation of regulations, but no danger to security since
the yard can be sealed off.

What is twenty-four dollars—one hundred and sixty
hours a month at fifteen cents an hour—to warrant such
risk? Just enough for cigarettes and some toilet articles,
but, in the context of endless petty harassment, too
much to surrender.

The warden comes out to the yard. With neither
apology for the mistake nor promise of correction, he
orders the men back to work. To his enormous surprise
they refuse to move, insisting that the pay issue be
settled first. The power binding the community has become too capricious. Other grievances find a voice. Visits
from single women categorically forbidden young and
predominantly unmarried men; mail allowed only from
immediate family; most magazines and papers pro-
scribed; these arbitrary administrative rulings undermine
the unspoken accord without which the institution cannot peacefully function.

The discussion on the yard escalates. Angered by the
warden's peremptory response to a fair complaint, one
prisoner says, "We want our money, warden. We were
sentenced to do time, not to be slaves." Furious at this
challenge, the warden shouts, "Damn it, you, I run this
institution!" "You ain't runnin' nothing' but your
mouth," another man shoots back.

Mad with anger, feigning compliance, the warden invites the prisoners into the main building to talk further. Once inside, however, he give a prearranged signal, metal doors slam shut, precluding retreat, and helmeted guards storm in from both ends of the corridor. When they first gathered, the factory men had agreed that their protest would be without violence. As they are clubbed down, no inmate swings back.

Learning what has happened, prisoners go wild, trashing cellblocks, burning mattresses, smashing windows. In doing this they surprise themselves. The jailhouse axiom is "Do your own time." Respect is accorded both fighting ability and the cunning to avoid foolish confrontation. To support the hundred men now in Isolation is not only to gain nothing, but also to risk paroles, hardwon privileges, and even physical safety. Nevertheless, prison wisdom to the contrary, the next morning when the work whistle blows few men move from their cells.

That day, and the day after, guards take more men to Isolation, hoping thus to break the spirit of resistance. They cannot believe their eyes. They have watched prisoners kill one another over the favors of a homosexual, they have encouraged race riots and tolerated food demonstrations, but never have they seen prisoners unite to protest their common condition.

By the end of the second day that the population refuses to work, the hundred single cells of Isolation are packed with three hundred prisoners. Paroles long gone, mutiny trials threatened, still the men persist, if only with the hysteria of those who know there is no going back. Hour after hour, day after day, they chant, beat on the bars, sing, and cheer.

Each successive morning the work whistle sounds. And each successive morning the men in Isolation, cheering, see through the bars of their cells and the barred windows of the block that again no one is going to work. More prisoners are beaten and thrown in the hole, the cellblocks are gassed and meals suspended, but the population refuses to work a third and then a fourth day.

Through the weekend, keeping all men locked in their cells, the warden searches desperately for "ringleaders." Snitches hand in every name that comes to mind, alleged organizers are interrogated, but no demon theory suffices. The truth is that the outside has at long last ruptured the seal on our timeless universe. Just as its hopes and techniques lose currency in the world beyond the walls, its leaders murdered or without influence, the civil rights movement breaks into our steel-and-concrete anachronism.

Long since, the rest of the country has begun to hear the rhetoric of revolution. In that rhetoric every man is a prisoner of the state, prisons the ultimate symbol of an oppressive system, prisoners its paradigm victims. But here inside the walls men have never heard the word "solidarity," they have no "class consciousness." An atrocity in a world of daily horrors has—to their great surprise—shocked them into common protest. Without any larger vision of what should or might be, still they persist, operating only with the knowledge that they cannot win.

On Sunday night in Isolation, the block flooded from water of stopped-up toilets intentionally overflowed, tear gas heavy in the air, guards and guardsmen in riot gear outside each cell of naked men, a prisoner begins to sing "We Shall Overcome." Though only now beginning to discover the bond of our common condition, in the face of the utter hopelessness of our situation, still we sing: ". . . deep in my heart, I do believe, we shall overcome, some day."

The following morning, hungry, scared, bribed by the warden's promise of no reprisals, without any faith or understanding from which to draw strength for further resistance, prisoners begin to return to work. From inside Isolation, through the several sets of bars we see them pass. Outside it is a bright and sunny day, not a cloud in the sky.

Young men of various races and some crimes, we in the hole are silent as the round of prison life begins again. Almost immediately it is as before, endless and without boundaries, the only rhythm there can be. So many removes from freedom, certain that worse is to come, we await the future naked to the whims of those in power, our cause futile, its essence still beyond our understanding, our lives in great jeopardy, our struggle unrecorded.

{{ornament}} {{ornament}}

Stumbling clumsily in our chains, we move through an incredible heat to file off the bus. This prison disguises itself as a Spanish mission, but inside, as we strip for yet another search, it is only more of the same. And then, abracadabra, we are again in cells, our metabolisms desperately braking from seventy miles an hour back down to suspended animation.

In the facing cell an emaciated Mexican looks up and across at me, his gauntness partially covered with a towel for a loincloth, an enormous crucifix on a silver chain concealing the cavity of his chest, pulling down his head. Like other Mexicans here, he is doing two years for illegally entering the country. Now, as time passes, neither able nor caring to speak English, he sits alone in his cell. Eating, sleeping, defecating, cleaning, waiting for men whose language he does not understand to abide by their own rules and set him free when the appointed days have accumulated. He waits, and trusts.

We regard each other for several moments. I throw him some tobacco and a packet of cigarette papers, which he sweeps into his cell with a broom. Unwilling to break off communication so soon, unable to decelerate enough to cushion my collision with stasis, still speeding, I venture a few words of Spanish.

"Yo no soy marinero, soy capitán," I say. He doesn't blink. "Venceremos." He makes no response.

I like the man, so small, so fragile, so childlike, so patient, so weathered. But there is nothing to say. Taking a last look at him, his brown skin, his ribs, the cavity behind the crucifix, I turn to my bunk, lie down, and pass the bitterly endless moments—one, another, another, and still one more—re-creating him from memory.

ૐ

Inside this Gothic fortress' massive brick walls, which preclude any view of a world too many removes away to imagine, much less actually see, there is this prison within a prison. In "segregation" there is little physical brutality. The burden is in being here, and in the bureaucratic power which determines the length and relative comfort of one's stay. Food, showers, books, writing materials, a walk outside the cell, return to the population, these "priviliges" derive from the Classification Committee, a body with all the power—but none of the safeguards—of the court it purports to be.

In one cell of this sanctum a Black Muslim interrupts his pacing to look up a word in his dictionary. Then he again walks five steps each way, back and forth, repeating the word. Playing no games with himself, he waits until he knows he owns the word before choosing another. As he resumes his pacing he shakes his head, impatient. He has no time to waste.

The Muslim finds himself in the hole because, arguing with the warden, he insisted that he had a legal right to receive the written materials of his faith. Indeed, a recent court decision enjoined officials of another prison from denying inmates just such writings. This warden, however, objects to the Muslim's use of the phrase "legal right." For the warden, what little inmates possess is a matter of privilege dispensed by grace, his grace.

Both he and the Muslim understand that in time the writ the Muslim has worked on so paintakingly will find its way out of the prison, one way or another, and that, after still more time has passed, a court will specifically extend its ruling on religious materials to this prison. The Muslim will then file a writ requiring the warden to show cause why he should not be "free" in the general population. Ten to fifteen months later he will be released from the hole, of course with no hope of making parole.

The Muslim has been inside the walls for ten years, and, long past the point of remembering life outside, dedicates himself to his faith. Muhammad offers both an understanding of the true nature of the universe and a regimen to transcend the schedules and incentives of prison. What a victory, for instance, not simply to refuse the pork other protein-starved inmates hunger for more of, but to do so armed with a knowledge that makes the sacrifice a gain. How sweet, to turn down so foul a bribe.

When not pursuing the dictates of his religion, the

Muslim follows a rigorous program of self-education. Among other disciplines he studies languages. Arabic, to better know his God. And English, to be able to outplay the monsters at their own game. The Muslim never stops studying the beast. Occasionally he can learn something new.

Across the corridor, behind the oaken door and wire mesh of the facing cell, a white man whose features the Muslim cannot quite discern ventures a conversation. At first the white-eyed devil warrants no response, but he keeps trying, his last gambit being to say that he has traveled the world. Putting down his book, moving to the mesh window of his cell, the Muslim asks the infidel, casually, just where he has been.

For the rest of the long afternoon and into the night, until the white man is taken to another cell, the Muslim listens to him describe city after city, experience after experience, speaking himself only to push the voice on, to allow no detail to escape. When the voice is finally arrested, the Muslim again paces his cell, not yet ready for sleep, testing his memory, reworking each image in his mind's eye. He redefines the stories he has been told, now walking those streets himself, slowly, in no hurry at all, savoring each city, each encounter, until he, as a man who had educated himself, as a man of the true faith, in fact possesses the experiences in a more real sense than the fool who only happened to have actually lived them.

In time, as he does his time, the Muslim will allocate the proper amount of time for those experiences to have been his own. One year for any other man, he'll figure.

Six of his ten years inside already liberated by this process of exchange, he will subtract one more from his term. Soon he will have done no time at all.

Down the corridor a man screams "Shame, shame, shame!" Some part·of the Muslim's busy mind confronts the cry, and, finding nothing of interest, files it for discard. A young white boy in a nearby cell, however, hears the words and labors to ward them off.

The boy is a draft resister, and feared at first that other prisoners would call him a coward. Times change, however, and now most inmates consider the boy no worse than a fool, a fool not simply for choosing to go to prison (for how could that beat the Man?), but a fool for getting thrown in the hole.

The boys sits in segregation, instead of working outside the wall with other "safe" prisoners, because his vision of resistance has led him to a policy of total noncooperation. He will do nothing, not even the token tasks the authorities assign to have all men appear productive. With the same purpose he refuses to sign any documents, and in failing to surrender his power of attorney can receive no mail. Without word from the outside, alone in his cell week after week, he communes with himself and with the shades of his memory.

Each day, three times a day, two guards open the door of his cell to give him food. And each day, three times a day, the boy makes a break for the door, and each time the guards pick him up, shove him back into the cell, and slam the door shut. The boy does all this to show that the government has no right to hold him, not so long as it wages this illegal and monstrous war. Time after time he screams that he will in no way consent to a government no decent human being could recognize as legitimate.

For the boy the fight against the war comes down to being pushed back into a cell by two men who have little understanding of why he makes them bother, except that it is a bother, and potentially dangerous to them. And the boy, alone in this prison within a prison, day after day, three times a day, makes contact with the war, with two prison guards who still one more time pin his shoulders and bind his legs. Six months down, four years and six months to go, it has already reached the point of insanity, yet the boy cannot relent: "You will not do this to me, or, if you do, it will not be with my complicity."

He goes for the door without even the prospect of anyone knowing the struggle takes place, doing it because he is certain it should be done, doing it also because now there is nothing else. Doing it perhaps never to say (or fearing that he will not, when it is all over, be himself to say): "This thing transpired, this is what I lived while you people moved on, this is what was eternal for me while you knew the truth and yet searched for revelation, this was my life while you postured and preened, costuming your struggles, God damn your pretensions and self-pity, what have you seen, where have you been?"

Every cell on either side of the boy, and all those along the line across from him, are occupied. No vacancies in segregation. All around his solitary struggle there is this community of sheer proximities.

Small gifts from the gods carry his neighbors' lives onward. One prisoner, finding a fragment of mirror, holds it through the mesh of his cell door as a window on the world, and expands his vision to include the guards on the corridor. A black militant at long last acquires a smuggled copy of *The Power of Blackness*, only to find that it is a study of the works of Poe, Hawthorne, and Melville.

Life continues within these limits, there is more of the same, and that is all there is, endless reaches of more of the same. Something at least one prisoner in the hole ponders when, viewing the murals of his mind, he lingers at a frieze of several figures, one the Muslim, and, nearby but quite separate, a struggling boy in the grasp of two larger men. Ah, there they are. Rigid. Fixed. Frozen. Still here.

﹏ ﹏

Clearly more diminished every day, Captain Jeff sits on the yard in the shadow of the wall, eyes downcast, oblivious of the flow of lives around him, saying not a word about his boat. Trapped and cornered too many times, having trapped and cornered himself too many times, now neither embattled nor inspired, he yields.

Perhaps it comes as a surprise to him that he is no longer a young man who happens to be passing through prison, one day to again be free and still young. Perhaps only now he perceives that parts of his life which seemed autonomous and secondary in fact partook of a primary whole. Suddenly imagining that he apprehends the pattern of his life, never before clear about the where-to of so many separate struggles and hungers, utterly dismayed by the revelation, Captain Jeff surrenders.

His demise began less than a month ago. A guard found him heading to work with a pocket Bible in his belt and confiscated it as contraband. Captain Jeff might simply have scored another Bible and concealed it the next day. But instead, true to form, he argued that no one could object to the Bible, and that there was no work to do anyway. Of course the guard refused to concede, so Captain Jeff, unable to let it go, demanded to be taken to the hole.

For several weeks he savored the quiet, meditating, enjoying this retreat from the hustles of life in the population. One day, as he was memorizing lines from the Sermon on the Mount, he looked up to see a group of middle managers from the local business community staring at him. "This is where we administer special therapy to disturbed inmates," a guard was saying.

Soon after, asked if he was ready to return to work, Captain Jeff informed the Lieutenant that things were just fine as they were. Outraged that Jeff had turned punishment to advantage, compelled under new regulations to issue full rations to all prisoners, the Lieutenant placed Captain Jeff's name on the change sheet for transfer to the central medical facility.

Though irritated with recent restrictions, the Lieutenant had learned that the psychiatrists would dispose of any human waste he sent them. A ticket from a prison to the medical center was nearly always one way. Or, if an inmate managed to struggle back to the comparative safety of regular incarceration, his medical folder carried plenty of Latinate reasons for placing him under closer "observation."

Getting the news, Captain Jeff was at first overwhelmed simply by the idea of transfer, any transfer. He had no heart for working through yet another labyrinth of pressures and dangers. Here at least he could give his adversaries a name.

As he thought about it further, however, Captain Jeff began to understand that at the medical facility he would never slide his way out of the psychiatrists' snares. Their presumptions would become his realities. To earn a release back to a mere prison he would have to prove himself "cured." And of what illness? Of having committed a crime and being caught? Of unwillingness to become what the prison authorities would have him be? Of subscribing to the heresy that he was sentenced not to change his being but to do time?

Yet if he resisted in any way, so many doctors around, nothing would be easier than to declare him insane and throw away the key. Or that might not even be necessary. Just the threat might push him over the edge.

Suddenly, being in the hole cell was no longer a refuge for Captain Jeff. Sweat pouring out of him, terrified, he began to race from wall to wall. Many times he had laughed at the confrontations he engineered, there was gallows humor in the ponderous responses of the guards when he provoked them, but it was true, he was locked into his pattern. He wouldn't work without his Bible, and if it wasn't the Bible it would be something else, something explicit, anything to insist on the difference between their rules and his life. And the guards? They could be trusted at least to notice and to report the acts of resistance from which he could not refrain.

Suddenly, then, as he shot back and forth in the tiny cell, the truth was unavoidable. The sum of all his possibilities no longer buoyed him. What he would have in the future was what he had now, just that, or less. All that had been and might be, all the promise and all the past, were now clearly beyond reach, and so, in an instant, both irrelevant and without existence. This was terminal now, even if he somehow stalled the transfer. No more open road, no more boat.

Without the possibility of getting out Captain Jeff has nothing to live for. It is the road, and being on the road, which is for him a metaphor for all that prison and the larger culture are not. How he savors the time he worked as a clown for a traveling circus, moving from town to town often without even a moment to get out of costume. Red lips, black eyes, tuft of hair on baldpate wig, large pants with balloon spots, and painted smile, he could give pleasure without yielding privacy. No one could see him, he did the right thing, and he was on the road.

Ultimately the circus folded, and he went down to Mexico, living by the ocean in a remote village, speaking only several words of Spanish, the Mexicans speaking no English. He passed his days in a hand-sign world where nothing could impinge on him, where there could be no obligation save the basic code of kindness to others. He banged his guitar and played with local children. No one told him what to do. There were slow days on the beach, fish fried on open fires, bad wine, and occasional Americans passing through.

Finally just too broke to stay, he drifted north. Dedicated to opposing the straight culture, too ideological to be a good criminal, picked up time and again for vagrancy, disturbing the peace, or shoplifting, he was at last nailed for passing bad checks. Asked by the judge if he had anything to say, unable to bear for another moment the endless hypocrisies of courtroom procedure, doomed and determined to speak his mind, Jeff told the judge to fuck himself.

Once behind the walls Captain Jeff fashioned a mode not simply for doing time, but for resisting the efforts of all others to bring him around to their points of view. He developed a vision of the future, a dream of the fishing boat he'd get hold of, something about twenty feet long with a small inboard engine, just powerful enough to chug him up the channel as Sunday boaters urged him to make way. He'd be down in the Bahamas, probably, in some little café, and on Saturday nights he'd join native friends to make some music. They'd sing songs with words he'd have no need to understand, they would simply share the warmth of good people brought together for an instant in time. When the moment had passed he'd return to his boat.

Living on it, he'd catch enough fish to afford tobacco and wine. He'd sell the fish to a local restaurant. Once a week he'd walk up the path with a sack on his shoulder and the owner would rush out to greet him, saying, "Oh, Captain Jeff, so good of you to come, just in time." And he would eat the meal as honored guest, once again fend off appeals for him to stay, and, finally, would sail off into the evening, a small dog his only companion.

Since I've known him, Captain Jeff has sustained this vision, self-consciously, deprecating himself by acknowledging that his dreams are dreamed, yet nonetheless insisting on the vision, seldom passing a tool, a piece of wood, or some scrap of metal without thinking out loud about what use it could serve on the boat.

Now, however, he sits silent on the yard. We know each other, Captain Jeff and I. Learning from him, I have tried never to tell him what to do, what to think, what to be, and he has returned the favor. Even when he

85

seemed sure to seal his fate, I held my tongue. Remembering that, trying to be courteous, he says, "You know, man, if I'm lucky, very lucky, someday you'll see me on a park bench somewhere, if they still have room for bums in this country by the time I get out, if I get out." As he thinks for a moment of just drifting, like the wind, a smile crosses his face.

Knowing what is true, however, without reason to sustain the struggle or the dream, Captain Jeff cuts loose his ties to the boat. Free, it wanders the sea without him, sails luffing, no one at the helm, bobbing aimlessly in the swell.

ॐ

Here, where everything is rendered unto Ceasar, officials guard against sins of omission in matters spiritual with a brace of authorized chaplains. Of the two, the priest is a Cadillac-driving alcoholic golf buff who treasures his memories of career military service. While aware that Christ died with a thief on either side, Father O'Rourke identifies his vocation with his rank. Consort of men in power, he wishes his flock amenable to the needs of his colleagues, the prison authorities. In his sermons, though mindful that all God's children have wings, he speaks not of Christ redeeming but of the Lord smiting the sinners.

The priest's Protestant counterweight is a short man with snake eyes, bulbous nose, dewlap-like jowls, and thin hair pomaded to his scalp. His tie barely reaches his sternum, leaving exposed an expanse of white shirt stretched to transparency over a massive belly. Here appearance is essence: sanctimonius and manipulative, the Reverend cashes in moral currency for secular influence in the institution.

Though he enjoys the exercise of power—and is often the harshest member of the disciplinary committee—the Reverend's true love is oratory. Generous to a fault, he offers a public-speaking class, mandatory for inmates selected by his friend, the Director of Education. "The Power and Pleasure of the Spoken Word" meets Monday and Wednesday nights after work. Prisoners go to the hole and forfeit paroles for refusing to attend these classes.

Central to the Reverend's mission are his welcoming speeches to new inmates. Stepping to the podium, placing both hands on the lectern, taking his time to show he is comfortable, gazing intently into the eyes of individual faces to "make contact," nodding graciously to the Captain, his host, the Reverend always speaks "off-the-cuff."

"Thank you, Captain, thank you very much. I'm glad to be able to be here with you today. It's always a great pleasure to share the podium with a man of your caliber." He bows slightly to the Captain.

"Men," he continues, "men, believe me, please when I say that you just do not appreciate how lucky you are to have this person in charge here. If you only knew." He sighs, rueful of so many lost opportunities.

"Well, men, though I know that you have much on your minds at this cruel moment, this, the beginning of your prison terms, nonetheless, let me be so bold as to impose briefly on your attention and patience, and perhaps, if one can hope, I can tender some small assistance to you in your hours of need.

"Now, some of you may wonder what the Reverend has to say to you. Indeed, I'll wager right now that some of you are probably wondering what an old goat like me is doing standing before you. 'Ah, he's over the hill,' you may be saying, or 'What can the Reverend teach me?'

"Well, gentlemen," he goes on, stressing the word "gentlemen," savoring his studied blend of irony and courtesy, "I may have one or two years on you, but let me say this, we're all in the same boat here. I tell you this in all candor. Now, some of you men may wonder, 'How can the Reverend say that we're in the same boat, what judge gave him his sentence?'"

Though such hypocrisy makes a mockery of his ministry, it in no way eliminates the need he might have served. Carved in stone high on the auditorium walls are these lines: "Whatsoever is brought upon thee take cheerfully and be patient when thou art changed to a low estate, for gold is tried in the fire, and acceptable men in the furnace of adversity."

More propaganda, but, to my surprise, the words strike a responsive chord. Surely we are being tried, and perhaps this itself dignifies our otherwise petty lives. If suffering brings man closer to God, then we are bound for Glory, even as here and now, in the swim of this prison life, we paddle like dogs to keep from drowning.

From inside the larger world fades until it is only a mirage on some far horizon. What was the stuff of life becomes the shadow play of "the streets," "my ol' lady," "my pad." Freedom, which we lose the capacity to imagine, comes to have meaning only in terms of not-freedom—release from this guard, that chow line, these walls. And when no such release is forthcoming, when life outside ceases to evoke any real feeling, then a hunger may grow for some larger deliverance.

In this vale of tears "Get-back is a motherfucker"; "What you see is what you get." Suddenly this is ordained, this is what you were heading for all your born days, we speak no longer of crime but of karma and sin. And then? Then release from this world without pity comes only through penance and the grace of pardon.

Time slows to a solid. Senses flattened by this corrosive sameness, I regress to increasingly simplistic modes of thought, I find myself ever more in need of certainty.

Just when it appears that my options have narrowed to either surrendering to the terms of this universe—and so abandoning any continuity with my past—or literally dying, I come across a newspaper article about the recently deceased guru Meher Baba. After many years of self-imposed silence, apparently, he finally "dropped his body." Not only does the phrase itself make me smile, but I'm moved by the confidence the words express, the faith that it is only the material plane that is being abandoned, so why worry?

Baba's cheerful belief in reincarnation and the existence of the soul advances me to deeper thought. If, as part of this life, prison can be transcended, then why not just slip into a lotus posture and leave it behind?

I try to envision the circumstances. One morning I fail

to show up for work. Guards come to my cell, and see in my place a cross-legged idiot who will never again enter "reality." Perhaps they'll ship this catatonic with my name off to the central medical facility. I myself, of course, will live on a higher and finer plane, whizzing round the galaxy with all the other souls freed from earthly burdens. Or perhaps before dropping my body I'll paint my lips with Day-Glo. If I also disincorporate as I change planes, then the guards entering my cell will find only a bright smile hanging in the close air.

Pretty thoughts, these, but the weight of this life leaves me full of doubt. To begin with, there's the possibility of failure. What if I miss, and in fact become a catatonic? That seems like loss, pure and simple. Clearly this plane-changing requires enormous faith. And doubt aside, what kind of choice is it anyway, made under such duress? I want to be here, and now; who wants to leave this earth? I just want to be out of prison, back with my friends.

Even as I take this tack I can hear gentle Baba admonishing me. "Come on, Thomas," he says, "it always comes down to this sort of decision. Sooner or later life fails one's expectations, inevitably there is the leap of faith." Perhaps Baba even serves up the hellish aspect of reincarnation, the fact that if I don't exert my faith now, then I'll just have to come back and do it all again.

Despite that risk, Baba's optimism to the contrary, I have an attachment to my life. I'm not from India, my way is all I know. Stir-crazed as I am, I'm just too bound to the material plane. I cannot willingly cut the umbilical cord which ties me to the only life I remember having lived.

Yet it is also true that within these walls there is only sadness and the prospect of final disintegration. And so I argue it back and forth with myself, alone in the night, I ponder the big questions, revolution to the left of me, astral planes to the right of me, still I try to choose, locked in some cell in some concrete ship on some barren and much eroded hill in the very middle of nowhere.

ನ≈

Though clearly we all share this misery in common, I labor to translate the truism into active sympathy. Were there only weekends off, annual vacations, some sanctuary or period of grace. As it is, however, one must fashion a psychic cease-fire zone without use of a white flag, and without promise of removal to the mainland.

Of course there are philosophies to console. It's this place which makes a man as he is, I suggest to myself, childhood training, racism, capitalism, or men may simply be handling their time the best way they know how. I run it up and down, but without trusting that I'll survive to look back on this time. Lacking that confidence, I'm left to dream how I might be, were there only a single moment to get out from under this enormous weight.

Dreams aside, I'm worn with the grayness of each slow hour, ground down by the noise, the routine, and the violence. I find myself slipping out of control, losing hold, backpedaling, now only reacting to each new assault.

It drives me wild, this place. Someone must put an

end to the blacks' endless verbal assaults. "Mother-fucker!" "Punk!" Someone, anyone, must silence the Puerto Ricans. "Chinga," "Maricon," "Vaya," hundreds of times each day, day in and day out. I need quiet. I must have quiet. Do what is necessary. Bind them. Tie them down. Cut out their tongues.

Weighing whether the Grenadier Guards or the Ton-ton Macoutes will handle this chore for me, I'm in the middle of a grin when Carl comes by. He says he's looking for some books to read, but we both know better. He wants company, and help. How to do his time?

Now here's a chance to set aside madness and self-pity and simply relate to a human being in need. But what clay Carl is! It isn't just that he has let himself deterio-rate in prison, putting on weight, wearing filthy clothes, wallowing in his own dirt, it is that one knows that things were never very different for him out on the street.

How not to insist on distance between oneself and this creature? How be so sure of survival as to afford the possible contamination of his self-abuse? Yet even as I imagine that I hang from the edge of some final preci-pice, still it is clear that Carl is not the enemy. Con-tempt is overkill to the threat he presents. Humor at his expense satisfies my need to differentiate between us, and Carl plays to it, though he insists one can push him too far.

Consider his bust, or his story about his bust. As he tells it, he was dealing cocaine (he would have been dealing a drug that inflates the ego of the user, he would have been dealing a drug carrying a mandatory five years, unparolable), and was lying on his bed one day when his partner came in. Though wiped out, he saw his partner drop a billfold onto the bed for him to look at. Opening it, Carl saw a badge. "Far out," he said to his partner, "where the hell did you find this piece of shit," and threw the billfold at the wastebasket.

Really loaded, Carl closed his eyes, and opened them again only when he felt a hand shaking his shoulder. As his vision cleared, he saw someone's legs. Still groggy, shaking his head, he slowly looked up, and saw, in this order, an erection pushing at the cloth of the pants, a hand with a badge in it, another hand holding a pistol with the muzzle pointing at his chest, his partner's shirt, his partner's neck, and his partner's face. His partner was the Man.

In itself, not a bad story, but Carl is too eager to please, encouraging men to laugh at him even as he is quick to be aggrieved when they take him for what he says he is. He also forces himself on others, telling blacks, for example, that he really understands where they are coming from, though in saying so he proves the contrary. Carl sets up his own falls. It's hard not to give him what he asks for.

Similarly, he professes an interest in the occult, and builds a contraband library of keys to the universe. Busy collecting and stashing new volumes, however, he has no time to ponder any one system long enough to fathom its teachings. Rather, he leafs the pages of each new testament, and then searches out the inmate acolytes of that particular faith, confessing to them that he just can't get into their trip, though they of course hadn't asked him to.

He does it all wrong, even to being the only man in the institution who wants the Sunday-night "luncheon meat," not only scarfing down his own portion but walking from table to table to ask hungry men for what they wouldn't dream of eating. Everyone waits for him to come by.

What, then, to make of Carl? I listen to his woes, offer some advice he can't hear, and watch him face his time. He has to do his nickel, there's no possible parole, no angle to play. And it is in this, in his response to the fixed term he must serve, that Carl comes into focus.

Responding to my suggestion that he improve his appearance, he says, "No, man, I don't start cleaning up till I've done half my bit." Carl has taken the jailhouse axiom to heart. "Break up your time," they say, so he's worked it out. He'll decay for half his sentence, he'll bring to perfection that part of himself which has always been his forte. And then, turning the corner, he'll begin to clean up and take off that weight, pound by pound, day by day, until he's down to within hours of freedom and, well, back to where he started.

At first it doesn't seem much to hope for, to finish one's time where one began. Many prisoners dream of picking up a skill to redeem the years inside. They'll learn to paint, to play the guitar, to sing, to hustle better, whatever, but they'll come out ahead.

Though some men take this as gospel, I can only view the time as lost, and, really, worse than that. The world is passing me by, I'm being unfitted for human company, so, given the flow in both directions, I'll be lucky not to take a loss on the future. It'll be something to get back to where I began this time.

For me, now, Carl's program makes good sense. He does have something to offer, then, and given his lack of malice, I'll build the bridge. Surely this is a devious route back to the human community, but it feels right. I'm just smiling to myself, I'm ready to say something more to Carl, anything, just to hear the sounds, but, sorry, he's got to split. You see, he's heard that someone has some Krishnamurti, and he wouldn't miss that to save his soul.

ॐ

Each weekday after breakfast Jack heads out to the rear sally port to wait for the morning search with the other members of his crew. Each time the nine men pass through the double gates—out in the morning, back in and out again at lunch, and in at the end of the day—all nine are frisked, and one is strip-searched.

Baring the anus, lifting the testicles, unlacing and re-lacing the work boots. Particularly in the morning, prisoners at the gate silently maneuver to avoid being chosen for the search. Actually, though, they have it easy. Were there more staff, and were the ritual exposure not so slow (palms, soles, hair, armpits, mouth, and genitals before the order to "spread your cheeks and crack a smile"), the warden would have every last inmate naked for every passage through the gate.

Though on rare occasions the guards turn up a letter

going out, or some jimsonweed coming in, everyone here knows that all serious smuggling is handled by the staff. Searches at the sally port, therefore, speak less to a fear of contraband than to the warden's uneasiness about having prisoners outside at all.

For the warden the goal is total quarantine, saving the free world from any contact with the diseases contained within the walls. Indeed, his view is not without merit, particularly if one assumes, as he does, that all inmates are essentially the same, defined by what the worst of them has done and by what any one of them might do.

Of course, few men here are incarcerated for crimes of violence; most of the violence inside occurs with the at least tacit approval of the staff; and what violence there is might best be said to inhere in or to be elicited by the institution itself. Perhaps the warden, knowing this, sees that *any* passage of inmates to the outside weakens—if only symbolically—the isolation from other life which alone allows the horrors inside even as it spawns them.

Why, then, does the warden let inmates through the gates, save to arrive in chains or to hurry out to freedom? Well, policy has it that the prison not appear "prison-like" when seen from the outside. Since there can be no shrubs or trees to give cover to an escapee, this policy translates into lawns. Lawns to mute the starkness of the walls. Well-manicured lawns to imply similar order within. As with nature, so with human nature. The lawn becomes propaganda, and prisoners simply the only available labor.

So it is that Jack and his crew tend this treeless expanse, keeping it green and, in a barren way, pastoral.

Armed with mowers, rakes, sickles, clippers, hoses, and sprinklers, they slowly circle the institution, returning to each section of lawn just before it becomes too difficult to cut. Each inmate works alone until the pickup returns with the ride in to the sally port.

If allowing prisoners to pass through the gates is contrary to the warden's sense of what's best, surely the passage out of and back into the institution is stranger still for members of the crew. From the outside the prison's gray bulk is lifeless. Massive walls muffle the din of fifteen hundred trapped lives. Not a soul can be seen. Wind blowing, sun shining, birds chirping, it is beyond imagining that, so close by, one man chases another through throngs of bystanders with the hope of splitting his skull.

Considering what's inside, working on the lawn should seem an improvement. Jack, for one, gets time alone, respite from prison's incessant pressures, and labor that is no worse than routine. Even so, the days outside pass slowly. Clouds glide by, a gopher burrows yet another exit. For men doing time, an important criterion is how fast that time passes. Even a dirty job can have merit if it anesthetizes the days, weeks, and months which build to the fulfillment of a term.

Further, each prisoner working outside is assigned a specific area, and any movement past its boundaries is considered an escape attempt. So circumscribed, though without visible restraints, the men stand, watch, and do not stray as staff and visitors come and go.

It is also true that from its totalitarianism prison takes not just its sorrows but whatever meaning it possesses.

Within the walls there is the consolation that life inside is the only life there is. To have to survive on these terms is not to be spared cruelty, but at least to be able to view it as what is. All other worlds are so far beyond reach that they bear on the inside only to make it seem lunatic and so more difficult to endure.

Nor does it help men working on the lawn to understand, perhaps after only one quiet afternoon, that the gains of days outside cannot pass walls impermeable to natural light and fresh air. What does survive re-entry is the knowledge that it is both unnatural and self-destructive to return inside at day's end.

For Jack long hours on the lawn leave him room to remember that he is party to his own demise. Here he stands in the sunlight, a man, so what holds him to this place? Why doesn't he take off? These questions nag at him even as he catches a frog, even as he maps hose attacks to drown yet another gopher.

One day, dropped down by the road far from the institution, watching the pickup truck and its AMERICA: LOVE IT OR LEAVE IT bumper sticker disappear around the bend, Jack is taken with the multiplicity of things. "Right now," he wonders to himself, tinkering with conundrums, "where is my wife, what is she doing? At the moment I think this thought, what is she thinking?" The day passing, in no hurry, Jack waits by the roadside for a revelation.

Finally, as the wind carries rasping words down from the gun-tower intercom, it dawns on him. What she is doing just then is living without him, still sharing his time, but trying to find a way in her heart to leave him and his slow death behind.

The day is very long. Jack's mind continues to wander. He is just realizing that nothing will return him yet another time to the sally port when, a hundred yards up the road, a car that had passed moments before stops and begins to back up. As it approaches, Jack sees—and notices that he sees—two things: the car is a maroon Mercedes sedan, and the driver is a woman.

Even as he watches the car draw nearer, it comes to him as if in a dream that the Big Bang theory makes sense. Of course all things in the universe were once compressed into a point the size of a pin, and, eons later, were dispersed in an incredible cosmic explosion.

As he sees the Mercedes' brake lights flash on, Jack further understands that the scattering of matter from that explosion will one day cease. Then the universe will begin to contract, ultimately once more collapsing into a single point, then exploding again, endlessly expanding and contracting in this timeless megacycle. And even as all this becomes clear to him, Jack also sees—in the last seconds it takes the Mercedes to reach where he stands with his rake—that the woman has come to make love to him and to take him away.

As the sedan rolls to a stop, the woman leans across the leather front seat to roll down the window. She is very beautiful, and her efforts tightens the blouse against her breasts. Certain he will explode, Jack hears her first words: "Excuse me, please, can you tell me the way to town?"

Staggered, but somehow finding the power of speech, Jack points up the road. "Just that way, ma'am, only a couple of miles," he says. Smiling at him, she replies, "Thank you very much," waves, smiles again, puts the sedan into forward and drives off.

Watching her go, universe imploding at a prodigious rate, Jack realizes that she did not even know he was a prisoner. In his tans he must simply have looked like an ordinary road worker. She was completely oblivious of what she might have meant to him. How could she have known?

Now again two worlds are one too many. In or out, whichever, but let one prevail. To escape, Jack heads down the road. Simple enough. To get back inside, however, he must wrest a transfer from the Captain, for whom, unfortunately, inmate assignments are forever. How, then, can Jack get a job change? Only by telling the Captain that he intends to escape, and so quickly being ushered off to the hole.

Throwing down his rake, looking around, walking back to the edge of the road, checking it out both ways, Jack turns, turns again, turns once more, and then, dizzy with choice, looking back over his shoulder one last time, violating all regulations by leaving his work area, he heads on up to the institution.

৯৯

One man stares out through a barred window at the ice-covered and barren plain that stretches away from the institution. Can he read something in that gray waste? Or is he just resting his eyes, for a moment sparing them sight of the lame, maimed, and crippled.

Look, there's Heinz, a stunted homunculus, face warped by a placating smile, achingly slow of thought, his spirit so broken that he will never lash out at those fortune made taller and more quick of wit. Look, twenty minutes before lunch Heinz shivers in the cold at the chow-hall door, a queue of one. He wants to be first at something.

Just across from the chow hall, inside the tiny shack thrown together to shelter the guard unfortunate enough to draw winter yard duty, old Docker stares blankly in Heinz's direction. A former fighter, now punchy, Docker cannot remember—even though his employee number is C-16—why they want him to say "CharleyonesixCharley-onesix" each time he checks into the institution.

Docker doesn't ponder what confuses him, he barely thinks at all, but he does feel. He's cold, standing in the shack. Does he understand that they've stuck him with the shittiest job? His nearly sightless eyes registering only occasional flickers of comprehension, Docker huddles in the wooden booth like a cuckoo in a tall and narrow clock.

Passing the guard shack and crossing the empty yard, a large and toothless inmate lines up behind Heinz. "Mongol" everyone calls him, to his face, too. While hardly an inventive nickname, it does fit. Forehead flattened, eyes slanted and close-set, webs reputedly connecting his toes, Mongol is a Mongoloid, all right.

They've told him that he's going home today. Though

for Mongol this prison life may be a kindness, he seems pleased with the prospect of leaving, if it's not imputing too much to him to say he can look forward at all.

Strange, that they bothered to lie; he won't be any trouble no matter what they do. Mongol has indeed wrapped up his time, under criminal law they can hold him no longer, but out at the front gate two psychiatric "attendants" are waiting. Mongol is being released from prison, but he's not going home.

A cold shot, really, even for a Mongoloid. And a bad omen, too. Think it over. What about Heinz, for instance? And old Docker, once he earns his pension. And, for that matter, anybody here, whoever they want, anyone at all.

෪

Another gray winter morning, sky low over the prison, only three hundred and four days till Christmas. Upstairs in the hospital, next to the centrifuge spinning down blood samples—plasma high, red cells low, white cells in between—the daily sick line forms. Some ill, some suffering the normal blockages of this sluggish life, some in search of a physical correlative to their miseries, the thirty-odd prisoners stand, one behind the other, waiting for the doctor.

Time passes. One older prisoner, clearly struggling to hold himself together, perhaps unwilling to fall apart without a responsible witness, asks the guard where the doctor is. "If he was up your ass you'd know." Indeed.

And why should the doctor hurry in? Just to wire more broken jaws, sew more torn anuses, and prescribe ever larger meals of Thorazine?

Down the hall from the sick line, Timmy, an inmate clerk, types up the doctor's notes on a patient: ". . . subject started at age ten to masturbate and continues twice weekly, but says in prison the sissies do it for him . . ." Having spent the last four nights terrified by hallucinations of clouds on the ceiling of his cell, unable to continue with the report, Timmy gets up and walks out past the sick line.

Heading on down the corridor, passing the security cell, he stops to look through the peephole. Each week, when, according to regulations, the doctor must re-examine all prisoners detained in the hospital, the man in this cell insists that he is not insane, that he has had no trial, and that he is the victim of a CIA plot.

Certainly prisons spawn both delusions and paranoia, but it is true, no inmate clerk has seen transfer papers for the man. Where did he come from? Where are they shipping him? Why the secrecy? Why isn't he in the population or down in the hole? What if he's telling the truth, wouldn't that explain why he set his mattress on fire, to get someone to listen and to help? Or is he just another complex psychotic, being moved in mysterious ways by the powers that be? Himself unable to trust that the guards won't one night abandon the institution, leaving the prisoners to starve to death in their cells, Timmy believes the man's claims.

Returning to his typewriter, spirits no higher for his tour of the wards, Timmy is just getting back to work

when Crazy Bill comes by. "Insist, consist, desist, sub-
sist," Bill hisses, "aware, beware, forswear, nowhere."
Timmy listens. "My poor friend," Bill says, "you are only
a tyro in this life, and you don't even know what a tyro
is." Crazy Bill's thing is words, and he fancies himself
crazy only north by northwest.

Each morning Bill comes around to offer Timmy the
benefit of his counsel. He does this because he's inter-
ested in Timmy, intrigued that Timmy considers himself
sane. Bill has never forgotten the day two years ago when
Timmy walked around the institution announcing that
he had made parole. Of course everyone congratulated
him, even the envious, and of course he was thrown in
the shower. And, according to jailhouse protocol, he be-
queathed his painfully acquired jailhouse treasures—pea
jacket, sweatshirt, and work boots—to those who would
have to stay behind. But then on the appointed day, lo
and behold, there he was, at work as usual. There never
had been a parole.

Amused by the discrepancy between Timmy's actions
and his self-image, savoring such assertion of sanity in
the face of this madhouse life, Bill decides to offer a new
clue to Timmy, who, Bill is certain, must be searching
for the Way. "Hey, home," Bill says, "lookee here. Listen to this poem I just finished. It's called 'The Turtle
and the Shark.' "

> The shark once asked the turtle for a ride across
>   the sea,
> The turtle said, "I'm sorry, I can't, it would be
>   the end of me.

You are, as you know, a shark," he said, "father
told me of your kind,
He said to stay far away from your type, and his
words still come to mind."

The shark replied, "I'm different, I'm your
brother, and a friend.
Besides, you're keen with wisdom, not like the
rest of them.
Take me across the sea," he said, "and you'll
see how fine I am,
Before I'd hurt you I'd cut out my heart, and
bury it in the sand."

The turtle said, "Okay, my friend, my brother,
let's begin,"
But no sooner had they left the shore when the
demon prepared to sin.
As they advanced on through the waves the
turtle was struck by pain,
The shark then took another bite, and said,
"My, what a shame."

Before the turtle died he heard the shark's voice
harsh and shrill,
"Why, never trust a shark, for it's his nature,
and he'll kill."

Message delivered, Bill waits impatiently for some re-
sponse from Timmy. "Obfuscation," Bill finally says to
Timmy's silence, "a panacea from Pandora's box."
Still saying nothing, Timmy looks down at the medi-

cal report on his desk. Another life suspended in time. Insomnia, loss of appetite, headaches, exhaustion. The feeling that everything is grinding to a halt. Violence in any direction. A beating. Rape. Self-mutilation.

Unrequited, Crazy Bill weighs Timmy's depression. He seems ready to stand by as Timmy goes under one last time. Or is he really trying to give Timmy a straw to grasp at?

"Hey, man," Bill says, "listen here. You tuned in?" Timmy nods. "Ready for this?" Timmy nods again. *"In nothing is no end,"* Crazy Bill says.

ॐ

They call me "kid." As I walk the yard, when I go to chow, as I return to my cell, I hear "How they treatin' ya, kid?" or "What's new, kid?" Only occasionally responding with some Stengelese, generally I linger for a moment and pass on.

"You shouldn't be here," they tell me, "a kid like yourself." "It's a rotten world," they say. They know almost nothing of my life, they ask to know nothing, but they are sentimental about youth. Though I feel aged past age, perhaps they are right. I look in the mirror. Hair cropped, face shaven clean, lines cleared by seven hours' sleep each night, no bills to pay, I hardly recognize myself. I am too young to be here.

Of course I do the same time they do, but it sustains us all to feel that we have the grace to wish things otherwise. If I should not be here, and they are human enough to know it and say so, then who are they to be doing time? Fathers of children, husbands of wives, family men, men good enough to want to see me free, why should men like this suffer such misery?

"It's a rotten world," I say when they tell me how they were done wrong. "Don't talk like that, kid," they respond, pleased, "you've got your whole life ahead of you." They do not want to see that I am dying, they would deny it, they perhaps never dreamed the dreams I know I am losing, they would prefer to believe there are things I cannot and do not feel, but they are glad I understand their problems, glad I commiserate. "They did you wrong," I say.

A delicate business, relating to these older men. Denuded without work and family, little sense of themselves internalized in their passages through life, they are terrified, and their assertions about the world in or outside become desperate demands for concurrence.

About their time, which must perforce be served, they are querulous, drawing me into arguments about legal trifles, badgering me to concede points I lack the power to grant. Searching for any mitigating circumstances, aching to be out of here, denied reprieve no conversation could bestow, they hurry away, bitter. And then, minutes later, they begin once more as they see me pass: "Hey, kid, what's happening?"

I can't give them what they need. My greatest obligation is to hold on for dear life to my understanding, lest I lose it and so forever lose myself. Always demanding white lies, they ask me to obscure what I struggle to clarify. And, threatened by any unfamiliar style, they are brittle, peremptory, their minds closed, much too much like the guards they hold in such contempt.

At the same time at least these men have lived some life, or have had some life lived in them. It sometimes seems that the younger men have done nothing but time. With the older inmates one can presume a richer past, and of course they live between past and future, unwilling to concede that the present is more than a brief detour from the real course of their lives.

A dentist serving six months for tax evasion describes his system for handling three patients simultaneously. An extortionist–gun runner shares with me cheeses he has bribed a guard to smuggle in for him. Giving me a cigar, he tells me—"in strictest confidence"—of secret meetings with Duvalier. And a stock manipulator recounts the beauties of his mistress. "You're never too old for it, kid, believe me," he says. He then explains how he has appealed for reduction of his three-month sentence by pleading the need to be at the side of his ailing wife.

This time is cruel on them. I should not set myself up as their judge. But still, serving short terms for lucrative crimes of financial deceit, they stand apart from the rest of the prison population. The younger men, for their reckless or desperate crimes of relatively small economic value, serve comparatively enormous amounts of time.

Though hardly responsible for the inequities of the world beyond the walls, many of these older prisoners are skilled exploiters, and bring their power not only into the courtroom but into the institution itself. An unfair example, no doubt, but I think of the sixty-year-old doing half a year for massive stock fraud. With his twenty dollars of commissary each month he can purchase the services of a young Honduran given two years for illegally entering this promised land.

As I look around me the young are dying, the old no argument for longevity. Just outside my cell an elderly man with a cane advances on a group of taunting middle-aged prisoners. Fat, bald, and gout-ridden, he moves clumsily, swinging his cane above his head, gasping with the exertion. His tormentors, who giggle like aged and distended adolescents, advance to just beyond his reach before withdrawing.

The old man speaks little English, but in any case his larynx is barely functional. The younger men mimic his grunts, laughing as he leans on his cane straining for breath. When he turns to his cell they rush at him again, throwing soap and towels at his back, waiting for him to turn, muttering to himself, to hobble at them once more.

All this is long since ritual, the opening calling for him to emerge bellowing at the sound of a shoe hitting his cell door. God only knows what the younger men take from this—the chance to bait an ogre, relief from the boredom of endless afternoons, or perhaps some kind of sexual release, so much teasing, all that chasing back and forth, back and forth—but the old man waits for them, this is the only attention he receives.

Even if one averts his eyes from such nakedness and from the future it augurs for oneself, the older men speak for still another negative possibility. Here every prisoner perforce makes some bargain with the institution. One man eats the food, another accepts a parole; whatever the terms there is always complicity. In their desperate refusal to concede that they are in fact prisoners, however, the older men become collaborators.

In some instances this makes for nothing worse than grim humor. The Lieutenant does his rounds, several older men circling the yard with him, perhaps believing that familiarity will give them some protection. Of course it is folly; the Lieutenant is a ruthless man. Some other older prisoners take front-office jobs, performing menial tasks for the guards and secretaries, hoping by proximity to appear part of the free structure of the institution.

Several older men actually become informers, but for most defeat is simply the steady denial of what is true. Surely it is a cruel reality, to be a prisoner is to be totally helpless, within such limits freedom comes only with the willingness to abandon all hope of release. With the willingness to die, really, since this is no kind of life. But what is the alternative? A guard complains that younger inmates don't fear time in the hole. Sympathetic, an older prisoner clucks his tongue. What's the matter with these kids? "Threaten them with transfer," the older prisoner suggests.

Another older man, who speaks only broken English, does his clerical work with lowered head, as if hoping to avoid any notice. He repeatedly fails to comprehend, or to acknowledge, the frequent insults of an Okie guard, who seems actually to believe that his own crippled utterances are the language of understanding.

Days pass, and often I see this man filing papers as though his life depended on it. Offended by the fear his pace implies, I speak with him. He tells me that one must always do a job well, any job. He also believes that the harder he works, the sooner he will be released.

The question of complicity means nothing to him. The only obligation, he insists, is to survive this place and leave it behind. Outside, there is the realm for choice. Irritated, I say that his efforts presume if not the fairness then the rationality of those in control, but that of course they are totally lunatic. Tears in his eyes, he tells me to leave him alone.

In the chow hall several days later he motions me over, offering me his portion of chicken. He doesn't eat meat. Always hungry, I accept, and in return search out contraband eggs and fruit for him. The exchange continues, but even as we become friends he will not believe that this life must be taken on its own terms. Each day, all through the day, he lives in a frenzy, forever hurrying the clock, anticipating every impending event, major or minuscule. "Pushing the time," he calls it.

Despite our differences we look out for each other. He worries after me, scolds and chides me, brings life down to basics. "What are you doing, wearing sneakers in the rain?" "Did you eat enough?" "How do you feel?" These questions, these questions. It seems so long ago that I felt such simple concern. These reminders of gentler times overwhelm me. With the kind and unthinking presumption that I might be in need, they pass right through the walls I have so painstakingly constructed.

Though he treats me like a son, I struggle to check my feelings. The crazed intensity of this world makes parody of all emotion. We need too much. Too far from life, we can only simulate and overstate what is real. And

111

still, I find myself so eager for peace that I enter adult-hood yearning to believe that a father, or a surrogate father, has power to save the child.

One night I fall ill. Swept into a fever, I feel his hand on my head as they carry me to the prison hospital. In my delirium, however, I understand all too clearly that it is not, really, a father's hand, it is too late. No, the hand is as spurious as the promise of release.

They wheel me through the double doors to a hospital cell, they lift me onto the bed and strap me down, and I cannot stop myself from saying to him, though he is not near me to hear: "Then tell them no more time, old man, if you have lived so long, you go and tell them no more time."

ॐ

Shorty and Al come by my cell to see if I have any smoking dope. "Say, man," Shorty says, "what you up to anyway? You writin' again?"

He watches me transcribe yet another moment of this life onto the page. "Sheuuut, Thomas," he says, "you know the Man just gonna come tear that stuff up and throw your ass in the hole."

I don't even raise my head. I have work to do, I'm busy, there's not a moment to waste. "Hope to die, Al-fred," Shorty says, as he sees I won't play, "if that boy ain't a writin' fool."

Shorty checks me out one more once. "Look at him go, Alfred," Shorty says. "Look at that. You tell me there aren't all different ways to do time."